Angela Howard grew up in rural Mississippi and was the only person in her immediate family to attend college. She currently holds a bachelor's degree in nursing and further certifications in medical case management and life care planning. Angela has begun a new journey as a motivational speaker to bring increased awareness of post-traumatic stress disorder (PTSD) in women and those who have suffered adverse childhood experiences (ACES). She is the founder of the PTSD-ACED Foundation, providing valuable resources to educators, healthcare professionals, and those who have endured ACEs. She resides in Memphis, Tennessee. *Sin Child* marks her debut as an author.

This book is dedicated to all of those who have been affected by adverse childhood experiences (ACEs) and post-traumatic stress disorder (PTSD), and to the people who care for them.

To Dr. *[illegible]*,

Thank you for all you do for others.

Angela Howard

Angela Howard

SIN CHILD

A Memoir

AUSTIN MACAULEY PUBLISHERS™

LONDON • CAMBRIDGE • NEW YORK • SHARJAH

Ordering Information:
Quantity sales: special discounts are available on quantity purchases by corporations, associations, and others. For details, contact the publisher at the address below.

Publisher's Cataloging-in-Publication data
Howard, Angela
Sin Child

ISBN 9781643787541 (Paperback)
ISBN 9781643787558 (Hardback)
ISBN 9781645365075 (ePub e-book)

Library of Congress Control Number: 2020900736

www.austinmacauley.com/us

First Published (2020)
Austin Macauley Publishers LLC
40 Wall Street, 28th Floor
New York, NY 10005
USA

mail-usa@austinmacauley.com
+1 (646) 5125767

First and foremost, I have to thank Neil White, author of *In the Sanctuary of Outcasts,* for encouraging me to write this book. He taught me a process of writing that was unique to my style and mentored me through chapters that I didn't think were possible for me to write. He was a careful listener and I could not have asked for a better mentor. Thanks to my friend and story editor, Kate Lechler, who believed in my story and spent countless hours with me helping to make everything not only come to life on paper, but also helping me see more deeply the raw emotions I constantly held as a child.

With much gratitude, I'd like to thank my dearest friend, Nancy Willis, for being not only my main editor but also my biggest fan. You were an invaluable supporter… always there and contributing endlessly in keeping me sane through the process of writing this book.

I would kindly like to acknowledge the various friends and their parents who provided me with shelter, food, and security when I had nowhere else to go, especially Vonda Flemons Winter, Alison Blount Nichols, Megan Bullock Grammer, Teresa Betts Collum, and others whose identities were changed in the manuscript for confidentiality purposes. Thank you to Megan Easley Thompson, the truly underserving brunt of my anger during high school, for teaching me the true meaning of forgiveness and compassion.

I'd like to thank the nursing professors and staff at University of North Alabama for going above their duty of teaching just nursing. They exhibited a rigid teaching process and expected perfection in every way. They were the first to push me to improve my English and writing skills, and those efforts made me not only a better nurse but a better speaker, a better researcher, and at the end of my career – a writer. Great thanks to all of the staff at Austin Macauley Publishers who believed in my story and made this book become a reality.

Finally, I would like to thank my two daughters, Katie and Chelsea, who gave me the courage and determination to pursue a greater purpose in life just by being in this world.

The Body: 1

I got the call that my mother had died on a Thursday afternoon in March 2016.

I was on my two-hour commute home to Tupelo from Memphis, thinking about the conversation I'd just had with my friend. We had grabbed lunch at the Belmont Grill after my last patient for the day, and she had shared with me how her mother used to scream when she ran out of Demerol, a pain medication with a high risk of addiction. Her story had reminded me of my own mother, Lisa, who had the same pill-addiction ever since I could remember. But I rarely shared this part of my life with people, preferring instead to keep a clear distinction between my past and my present. Lisa was in the past. She couldn't hurt me anymore, but that didn't mean I wanted to talk about her.

Half way home, the name 'Granny' lit up the screen on my phone.

I could count on one hand the number of times that Granny Jack, my mother's mother, had called me during my entire adulthood. Every call had brought tragic news. I wondered if she was calling about Paw, my grandfather, whose health had been fading swiftly due to throat and neck cancer.

Worried, I answered, "Hello?"

"Hey," she responded. She sounded gruff, as usual, but also slightly shaken. "What's wrong?" I asked.

"You know Lisa's husband, Big Mike?"

"Of course." Mike was Lisa's eleventh husband and had been in and out of her life since I was twelve years old. He was called Big Mike because he was six-feet and seven-inches tall, and weighed over 500 pounds.

"He's been in the hospital for about ten days," Granny rattled on. "They say he has sepsis and it don't look like he's gonna make it."

While she talked, I wondered why she seemed upset about Mike. Granny Jack had never liked her own daughter, much less Lisa's various husbands. Why did she care? And why was she calling me to talk about it?

"Well, your mama, she hasn't been to the hospital to see him in days."

This didn't surprise me. Lisa had proven time and time again that she was not someone to be depended upon. When I was six, she abandoned me with my great-grandmother, Memaw, for three months. And at fifteen, when I was hospitalized with pneumonia for a week, she didn't even bother visiting me.

"Well, that's not a shock," I said. "You know how she is. She has never really cared about—"

"She's dead," Granny Jack interrupted. "Mike hadn't been able to get her on the phone for three days, so he sent someone to check on her. They found her dead in the house. Said the body was already decomposing."

My hands began to tingle and my legs felt weak.

"What? Are you sure? Who told you this?" I asked, disbelieving.

"I talked to the cops. She's at the Jones County Morgue in Laurel. I figured you should know."

I waited for Granny Jack to continue, wondering if she would ask how I was doing, how this news made me feel, anything nurturing or grandmotherly. That expectation was cut short with her next words.

"Alright, Angie. Bye."

I looked at the clock. The phone call had lasted no longer than three minutes. Another five minutes went by before I wondered if I should let anyone know. The last I heard, Lisa's only other children, my half-brother and sister, Scotty and Niki, were both in prison for the second time, Scotty for armed robbery and Niki for drugs. Did they know? How could I get in touch with them?

Something stopped me from trying to contact them, though. Lisa was a habitual liar, manipulating everyone around her to get what she wanted. I didn't know how, but I felt that this could be another ruse, another prank.

I would have to go see for myself.

Chapter 1

Bastard, you damn bastard!

Nose to nose with my stepfather's pet boa constrictor, I felt like I was screaming these words, but only my panicked breathing could be heard over the snake's hiss. I wanted to block out Boey's flickering tongue, its body coiling like black lightning with excitement for its next meal. But each time I made a noise or cried one tear, my stepfather squeezed my neck harder and shoved my face farther into the metal trunk where the snake was kept. So I screamed in silence, a terrified child, not sure if my words were directed to the man or the snake.

Whenever my stepfather felt the need to threaten me, he pushed me up against the side of the trunk to watch him feed Boey, holding a rat by its skinny tail.

"You see that?" he asked. "He's hungry. Do you see how hungry Boey is?" Once Boey had eaten and I could see the outline of the rat in the snake's body, he whispered in my ear, "I will lock you in this cage with Boey and after it eats you, I will feed your mama to it, and then your memaw. That's what I will do if you ever tell anybody about me and you." He demanded an answer. "Now tell me you ain't never gonna say nothin'. Say it. Now!"

"I promise," I whimpered. "I promise I will never say anything."

***

When I was six, I lived with my mama, my stepfather, Jerry Bramble, and my brother and sister in the projects not far from the train tracks that ran through the woods outside of Okolona, MS. We lived with Jerry's mom in her brick two-bedroom duplex that had two window AC units, a luxury compared to most of our neighbors. But inside there wasn't much luxury. White tile floors, stained yellow from cigarette smoke, and not enough beds to go around, especially when Jerry's sister or brother came to stay with us, bringing along an assortment of cousins. We made pallets on the floor, laying down tattered quilts and crocheted afghans for all the children to nest in. On most nights, you could find anywhere from six to ten kids sleeping there, with adults in the real beds or on the couch in the living room.

I was the oldest of three half-siblings. I barely remembered my daddy, Eddie Leech, other than a faint impression of a tall, broad man with a perfectly manicured mustache and goatee. My four-year-old brother Scotty was Carl Proctor's son. Every time Carl came to visit, no matter how kind he was to me, I worried he would take my brother away for good. Scotty took after his father, with his dark brown hair and sweet expression. I never knew why my mama and Carl had split up, but I knew he was better than Jerry, my mom's third husband.

Jerry Bramble worked at a local furniture factory as an upholsterer. At six-feet tall, he towered over me, a strongly built man with red hair, a scruffy beard, and a mustache. I was terrified of him, of his pet snake, of how his Adam's apple looked like it took up his entire neck. But my mama, Lisa, had married him when I was four, and together, they had Niki, my two-year-old sister.

Mama was one of the most beautiful women I had ever seen, and she had always attracted others. Despite smoking and tanning, she had a flawless olive complexion, slightly freckled but without a blemish and always silky smooth. Her brown eyes were deep-set into her long, narrow face, framed by beautiful dark auburn hair. She was tall and slender and could turn on the charm in an instant, getting men and women to do exactly what she wanted.

"You can get whatever you want in life if you please the right man the right way," I heard her brag on more than one occasion. Men flocked to her, showering her with gifts, money, pills, and their attention. She had no problem getting out of paying overdue bills and most of the time had a sports car, convertible, or high-end luxury car. If she got caught speeding or driving under the influence, she could turn tears on and off like a water faucet.

I adored and feared Mama. When she was in a good mood, I was her little girl, her "Pangie Bear," someone she could rely on to get her pills or a glass of sweet tea, or make a lunch of pork 'n beans for my little brother and sister. She would laugh with me about the people she scammed. I wanted her to like me, to be on her side. But at the same time, I felt uneasy, afraid each time she weaseled her way out of something. I worried that I would say the wrong thing, stressed that I would accidentally reveal a lie she had told. She coached me on what to say to certain people, but instead I found me making myself scarce, refusing to speak at all if we were in a place where people knew her.

If I made her mad, I knew what the consequences were: screaming, cursing, and throwing things. If she was out of her prescription drugs, the punishments were worse. She might hit me with a hairbrush, or hold a hot iron over me, or burn me with cigarettes. When she had a wild look in her eyes or an edge to her voice, I could tell that something bad was about to happen.

It didn't usually happen to Scotty or Niki. Carl Proctor wouldn't tolerate Lisa abusing Scotty, and she never hit Niki when Jerry was around. At the most, she might give Niki the first pop with the belt, then one loud pop to Scotty. So Mama took most of her anger out on me.

"Now it's your turn, you little wench! I hate your stupid guts!"

She gave me repeated licks with the belt. When she threw it to the floor, the real punishment began. Using her hands to hit me and pull my hair, she shoved me into the corner of the living room. "Now you stay there! And keep that ugly-ass face pointed at the wall. I don't want to see it look up!" Sometimes I had to stay in the corner so long I wet my pants or vomited. But I always forgave her. *She didn't really mean those things*, I told myself. *I'm just unlovable – a horrible person who deserves to be punished.*

So I didn't tell her what Jerry did to me, thinking that it would only add to the list of reasons for Mama to hate me.

Chapter 2

When other people were around, Jerry Bramble treated me like I was dirt. One Valentine's Day, when I was six, Jerry came home from work with lots of balloons, a huge stuffed animal, candy, and flowers. We rushed outside to greet him and he distributed the gifts right there in the parking lot to Mama, Niki, and Scotty. I waited eagerly for my present – a big box of chocolates or some balloons, I hoped.

But I was disappointed.

"Bad girls don't get Valentine's presents," he said gruffly, giving me nothing. I turned away and walked toward the end of the apartment building close to the noisy four-lane highway.

"I don't want anything from you anyway, you bastard," I mumbled under my breath, using the word Mama always used toward people she really hated.

When no one else was around, though, Jerry felt freer to hurt me. One of the first times I remember happened at Memaw's house.

Lora Bell Barker was Mama's grandmother, my great-grandmother. She was only fifty-three when I was born and, as her first great-grandchild, I had given her the nickname Memaw. She worked in the manufacturing industry, first sewing denim jeans, and then later sewing seat cushions and backs for stationary furniture. Her youngest daughter, Deb, was born with severe cerebral palsy, still lived at home with her. Despite spending long hours at the factory and then coming home at night to take care of Deb, Memaw's gentle touch felt as if it could magically heal my deepest wound.

Every time Mama was in trouble, we went to Memaw's. She lived in a cozy grey-brick house right on the corner of Church and Silver in Okolona only two or three blocks from the projects where we lived. Sometimes we stayed there for weeks at a time while Mama dealt with her current crisis, whether it was forging checks, slashing someone's tires, or not paying drug dealers for pills she had bought. Memaw didn't turn anyone away; even Mama's current husband or boyfriend was welcome to stay with her. I loved being there; most of the time, I felt so safe and at peace – but not always.

"I have good news," Lisa announced one evening when she got home to Memaw's. "I got a job at the Junior Food Mart today. I'm starting tonight!"

"That's good, Lisa, but I won't be home to watch the kids," Memaw said. "It's Saturday and I always go to the VFW on Saturday nights."

"It's okay, Jerry said he would stay with 'em." Mama turned to me, "Angie, come over here and give Daddy Jerry a hug."

Somehow Mama knew I didn't enjoy being around Jerry and enjoyed watching me squirm with discomfort. I'm not sure I understood the reasons for my feelings at the time. But my heart pounded and my feet felt like they were weighted, bolted to the ground and couldn't move. Instead, I ran to the front yard, pretending that I didn't hear her words. Scotty joined me and we played outside until it was time for Mama and Memaw to leave.

I went to the bathroom in the middle of the hallway where Lisa was getting dressed.

"Mama, please don't go to work tonight," I begged. "Can't you stay home? I promise to be good. I'll take care of Scotty and Niki so you don't have to."

She stopped buttoning her blouse midway and charged at me. "Get the fuck away from me before I beat the shit outta you!"

Since that effort failed, I followed Memaw to her bedroom. I held my breath as she put on a pair of long turquoise earrings set in silver.

"Memaw, you can't go anywhere tonight," my voice trembled and I felt a sudden panic welling up inside me. "You have to stay here with me. Please don't go. Please."

But the voice that always comforted me struck me like a bolt of lightning.

"Baby, I need to get out of the house for a while and have some fun with folks my age," she said. "I won't be gone long. Your daddy Jerry will look after you, and your brother and sister until I get back."

I ran to the front door and escaped the house, staying outside until they left. I watched them drive away in separate cars and I wished I could run as fast as that, to follow them down the street with my bare feet. I sat down in the driveway and began tossing small pebbles out into the street in attempt to keep myself from crying.

The sun had set and the sky was getting darker. I heard footsteps approaching from behind and smelled cigarette smoke. I jumped to my feet and started to run, but was halted by two masculine arms wrapped tightly around my waist. I tried to wrestle free from the grip.

"Where you goin' in such a hurry?" Jerry taunted.

I didn't bother to answer, instead giving him the most evil look I could muster. "You and me, baby Niki, and your little brother gonna have us a big time tonight," he smirked. "I know you missed me while I was gone."

I wanted to spit right in his face, or take the grit and pebbles I had been sitting amongst and throw them in his eyes. He kept whispering, his tobacco-filled breath spilling into my face.

"I'm gonna be the king and you… you gon' be my queen."

He led me into the house and to the dining room where he pushed me down onto to the floor next to the large mahogany dining table. He called Scotty into the room as he lowered himself down to the floor next to me.

"Now son, we're gonna play a game," Jerry said. "I'm the king and you my servant. You gotta go in the bathroom with Niki and shut the door. You get a whole dollar if you don't come out until I call for you. You think you can do that for your king?"

Scotty stood over us with a puzzled look, but was delighted at the thought of getting an entire dollar. He took Niki and raced out of the room. A chill ran down my spine as I heard the bathroom door slam. My breathing grew heavy and I felt lifeless, as if I could feel my consciousness slowly drifting from my body. In my mind, I could hear the sounds of the hissing boa constrictor, just like I was next to it, but it wasn't there – it was back at our house in the projects.

The streetlight peered in through the window from the back yard, but I only saw darkness. I felt a crushing weight on top of me. To this day, I don't know exactly what he did. All I know is that I felt a ripping pain between my thighs up to my stomach. Although I envisioned myself screaming for help, begging him to stop, no words actually came out.

Soon it was over. Jerry called for my little brother to come out of the bathroom. Scotty collected his dollar and fell asleep in my arms on the living room couch. I pretended to be asleep until Memaw got home late that night. When I finally got behind the closed door of her bedroom, I was relieved.

Chapter 3

All I knew about sex when I was six was what I learned from Mama. I had overheard her phone conversations with men, and had even walked in on her in the act several times. But I thought sex was supposed to make you feel really good, so I didn't connect it to what Jerry had done to me, which had been the most painful, horrible event in my life so far. I also didn't know why Granny Jack, Mama's mother and my grandmother, constantly referred to my mama as a whore, a word she applied to everyone from the 'lot lizards' she ran into at truck stops to her own teenage daughter, Kim, who had gotten pregnant twice in high school.

But I was starting to see a pattern. Even though Scotty and Niki got to stay inside, Mama often locked me out of the apartment in the projects during the day. While she was inside, I sat on the concrete steps outside the back door, crying so hard that I felt like I was going to pass out in the humid summer heat.

"Please, Mama, let me in," I begged, banging on the door, my long hair so wet with sweat that it wrapped around my face and arms like twine. "I promise I will be quiet and won't say anything!"

It never worked. At best, she ignored me. At worst, she came to the door to threaten me or hit me in the head. "I'm gonna beat the hell out of you if you knock on this door one more time!" she said. "You are not comin' in while I got company. Matter of fact, you ain't comin' in when I don't have company."

The company she entertained was men – three different men in particular, but never on the same day, and never when Jerry or his mother were at home.

When she slammed the door in my face, I ran away, internally screaming the two words I had learned to connect with Mama: "Fucking whore!"

Locked out of the house, the only people looking out for me were the other residents of the complex, all of whom were black. Most of my days were spent on the playground that stood in the grassless circle in the center of the projects. Every back door in the inner ring of the apartment complex led straight onto this playground, and other kids came and went throughout the day, swinging on the tall swings, going down the two long metal slides, or playing tag on the monkey bars. During summer months, it didn't take long for me to become sweaty and covered in dirt from the playground and metal play equipment. I never told anyone I had been locked out of my own house – I was too embarrassed – but some of the children must have sensed it. They often invited me into their homes for a snack or a drink. Their moms fed me lunch, sometimes breakfast, too, if they saw me early enough. They bathed me and washed my clothes, letting me wear their children's clothing.

One of the mothers, Miss Janet, had the most beautiful skin I had ever seen. It was dark and gleamed like satin, perfectly smooth, without a blemish. She had dimples and a twinkle in her big eyes every time she smiled at me.

"Now baby, you just sit yourself right down here at this table and eat," she said, hugging me. "All these other young'uns are eating, and you might as well, too."

Those words coming from Miss Janet always made me feel good, like I was safe and valued. She was kind and loving, stern but gentle, the kind of person you knew you could rely on, the kind of mother I wished my own Mama would be. I didn't allow myself to get too close to this woman, though, or any of the other families. I was afraid my mother would dislike me even more than she already did if she thought I was more fond of someone else than I was of her.

Nobody in my life thus far had treated me with such routine kindness. Other than my great-grandmother, who was sweet but didn't have the spirit to defend me against Mama, the other women I grew up with were hard women. Granny Jack, for instance, was about five feet and two inches tall, 120 pounds of pure brass, and the only female truck driver I had ever seen. She could back a fifty-three-foot trailer down the narrowest alley in New York City and she never hesitated to put people in their place, at times backed up by a knife or gun. Her fearlessness meant she wasn't afraid of mafia members or drug lords, and certainly wasn't intimidated by her wild daughters, Lisa and Kim. She once threatened to hang her first husband, my biological grandfather, in the presence of FBI agents who were investigating him as one of Mississippi's 'most wanted.' Family legend had it that she stabbed her second husband in the stomach three times, with the excuse, "I found cigarette butts in his ashtray… but the lipstick wasn't my color!" She took great pride in her fighting nature and would often brag, "Just ask anybody in the whole damn town of Okolona who the meanest person they know is… they'll tell you real quick it's Jackie Reed."

Mama had inherited Granny Jack's temper and so, it seemed, had I. I was angry all the time – usually at Mama. When she punished Scotty and Niki, I would cry tears of rage, unable to keep the tears from falling. When my efforts to gain her love and attention failed, I ran out into the woods to scream and throw rocks at trees. I never yelled at Mama's face, but behind her back I cursed her. Cursed her for hitting me, for hurting me.

Cursed her for not loving me. Cursed her for loving everybody except for me. So I learned to express myself in anger rather than in softness.

Chapter 4

When I started kindergarten at Miss Jackie's preschool in Okolona, my only friend was my distant cousin, Renee. Renee's grandmother and my memaw were sisters. She was a scrawny girl, with pale skin and white-blonde hair that hung just past her shoulders. She was hilarious and very protective of me. We played together at school and sometimes I spent the night at her house, which was just down the street from Memaw's.

Her family was different than mine, though. Her father, Jerry, was an officer in the army, and ran his house with military precision. Renee was often punished if she forgot to address her parents as 'sir' or 'ma'am.' Her mother, Sue, on the other hand, had a thick Northern accent, a flirty personality, and cooked delicious, well-balanced dinners that the family shared together each night.

Part of me was jealous of Renee for having such a life. Another part found the perfection of her household – the manicured lawn, the place settings at the dinner table – too much to deal with. I was used to eating meals of potatoes, pork 'n' beans, and biscuits at various times, in front of the television or back in my bedroom, my plate propped up on a towel. I poked fun at Renee for eating her vegetables –

glowing orange carrots, dark red beets, half-cooked broccoli – so faithfully.

"No damn wonder you're so pale, you gonna turn orange if you keep eatin' shit like this," I teased her, then forced her to follow me outside to dispose of the beets I'd stuffed in the pockets of my khaki shorts. We took turns throwing them at the neighborhood cat-lady's porch, watching as hordes of hungry felines descended on the vegetables.

"Look at 'em, they're eatin' that shit just like it's tuna!"

"Angie, you shouldn't say that word!" Renee said, laughing. I just smirked in response, and said "shit" again.

I was used to being a bad influence. Despite the efforts of my kindergarten teacher, Miss Wilma, I used bad language all the time; four-letter words were a natural part of my vocabulary. I also liked to fight with boys on the playground at recess, feeling the need to prove I was as tough as the other women in my family.

One day, I took a boy down and a rock ripped his knee open. He lay on the dirt playground and wailed in pain.

"Get your ass up off the ground and be a man," I yelled at him. "Stop actin' like a little wussy!"

The other kids ran and told Miss Wilma that I called the boy names. She put me in time out and made me sit behind her desk at the front of the classroom while she took care of his wound. It felt like an eternity until she came back to talk to me. She sat down next to me with a serious look on her face.

"I didn't mean to hurt him that bad," I told her.

"I know you didn't mean to hurt him, Angie," she said in her gentle voice, "But why did you start calling him names after you knew he was hurt?"

"Because he was being a little wuss. He's just gotta learn to have some balls, Miss Wilma."

She tried not to laugh, but a chuckle escaped her slight frame.

"Sweetie, I know you hear a lot of things at home, but I want you to know it's okay for people to cry sometimes, especially when they are hurt," she said, her face serious again. "Strong people can cry, too. People as strong as you, even."

This advice didn't make much sense to me at the time. Crying wasn't strong. If it was, why did Granny Jack, the strongest woman I knew, have a steadfast rule of 'no crying?' Why would Mama, who only respected people who were tough, sometimes hit me harder if I cried? When I found myself getting teary-eyed for any reason, I had a habit of excusing myself to go to the bathroom, staring at my reflection in the mirror until there were no more tears in my eyes.

Miss Wilma pulled me over next to her and sat me on her lap. "You are a strong girl. And, deep down, you are one of the sweetest little girls I have ever seen. Miss Wilma loves you and I want to see you always show other people that goodness that I see. And," she said warningly, "I don't want to hear anymore ugly words come out of that pretty little mouth. Is that a deal?"

"It's a deal," I said reluctantly. I knew I had to prove myself to be tough at home, but maybe at school I could try to be a good girl, on my best behavior. After that, I offered to help her clean up the classroom at the end of the day, wiping down the chalkboard and taking out the trash.

"For one so ornery, you sure are sweet," she told me, thanking me for my help.

Even though she spent most of her days correcting me when I cursed or got into fights at recess, I felt that I was Miss Wilma's favorite student. She never let on that she knew anything about my family, but she sensed that I needed extra help. I even began to spend weekends with her, making banana splits and going shopping at the old Sears Mall in Tupelo. Once she bought me a Barbie, a gift I treasured. Somehow, Miss Wilma had seen underneath my hard, 'ornery' exterior and chose to nurture sweetness instead.

Chapter 5

Early one morning, the summer after kindergarten, I saw Mama packing things in suitcases after Jerry left for work.

"Are we going somewhere, Mama?" I asked.

"Hell, no, we ain't goin' nowhere. Now mind your own damn business and go fix your brother and sister some breakfast." She rushed us through the meal, then ordered me to get Scotty and Niki into the car.

"I've got to get groceries," she said. "There's not enough room to fit the groceries with us in the car, so I'm gonna take your brother and sister with me, and drop you off at Memaw's."

It was almost 8:00 am and Granny had long been at work. Lisa pulled the car under the open carport on the side of the house and I climbed out. She ordered me to sit on the grey brick steps leading up to the door.

"Now you stay right here in this carport until I get back. Don't you leave and go nowhere. You hear me?"

"Okay, Mama. Will you be back real soon?"

"I'll be back to get you in a little bit," she said coldly. "Say bye to your brother and sister."

I felt an immediate sense of dread as the music blaring from her black T-top Trans-Am faded into the distance. The air was so humid I felt like I could hardly breathe; I wanted to vomit. My bare feet burned every time I walked across the hot concrete. When Memaw finally arrived home for her lunch break at noon, it felt like I had been sitting on those doorsteps for hours.

"Mercy, baby! What are you doin' out here in this heat?" she asked, stepping out of her yellow El Dorado.

"Mama had to get groceries," I explained. "She's comin' back to get me in a little bit."

"How long have you been sitting here? Your face is blistered." Memaw reached for me and hugged me, burying my head into her stomach. "Now let's go in the house and get you cooled off."

After getting me a glass of ice water, we walked down the narrow hallway to Debbie's bedroom.

"Look who I found when I got home," Memaw said as Debbie smiled at me. "Now you stay in here with Deb and drink your water while I make lunch."

When Memaw came back, she had two plates and a wet washcloth. She sat one plate on the table in front of Deb and the other plate on the perfectly made twin bed where I was sitting.

"Now let Memaw wash you up with this cold rag," she said, wiping my face and hands, then placed a folded wet cloth on the back of my neck. Then she began to feed Deb lunch.

"Lisa done lef' her again?" Deb asked in her broken speech.

"She'll be back," Memaw said. "I just hope she hasn't gone and got herself into trouble."

I didn't know why, but this made me nervous. I could barely finish the rest of my lunch.

"I've got to go back to work," Memaw said. "You stay inside and take care of Deb for me. I'll be back as soon as I get off work. I promise." I followed her to the door and waved good-bye as she backed out of the driveway.

The afternoon lingered on. I watched every window for signs that Mama was coming back. While Mama had no problem dumping me off onto other people for an afternoon or a night, like Renee's family or Miss Wilma, she had never left me without an adult to hand me over to. I worried something had happened to her. Had she been in a car accident? Did she run away? Who would feed Scotty and Niki?

Memaw kept her promise and came straight home from work.

"Has your mama been back?" she asked as she began to cook supper. I shook my head, trying not to cry.

All that evening, I kept watch for Mama. I stood at the tall picture window in the living room studying the shapes of cars passing by in hope that the next one might be the Trans-Am. I focused so hard on the next set of headlights coming down the road, I barely heard Memaw when she spoke.

"It's time to get you a bath and go to bed, baby," she said. "Angie, c'mon, let's go to bed. There's no need to wait up any longer."

"I want my mama!" I began to sob. "She told me she was comin' right back!" Memaw's strong arms grabbed me from behind, hugging me to her chest.

"You've fretted about your mama enough for now. Wherever she is, she's alright, and she'll be back. She'll be back when she's ready, baby."

She dressed me in one of her soft, flannel pajama tops, rolling the sleeves up past my elbows, then pulled the large down comforter over both of us. "Put those little warm feet on Memaw's cold legs," she said, then read *The Little Engine That Could.* I fell asleep listening to her soft, animated voice, studying the gold foil spine of the book.

The next morning I woke to the smell of homemade biscuits and bacon cooking. I leaped out of the bed and ran down the hall into the kitchen.

"Is my mama here yet?"

"Not yet, baby. Here's you a hot biscuit." Memaw was good at changing the subject of tough conversations to food.

It had been nearly two months and Mama still hadn't come back. Although I still spent a good amount of time at the front window, watching the road, I developed new routines with Memaw and Deb. While Memaw was at the factory, I watched *Days of Our Lives* and ate Hershey's Kisses with Deb, or went outside to play with the neighbor kids. When she got home from work, I watched her take care of Deb's needs, feeding her, lifting her from the day chair to the bedside toilet, to the bed. Once Deb was tended to, Memaw tucked me into bed. Sometimes, though, a feeling of dread would engulf me and I could envision the three of them – Mama, Scotty, and Niki – lying in a ditch underneath a flipped car, their bodies rotting like the ones that I had seen in horror movies.

Late one evening, the phone rang at Memaw's house.

"Lisa, is that you?" I heard her say. I ran from the living room into the kitchen and saw Memaw holding the yellow receiver from the rotary telephone that hung on the wall.

"God Almighty knows, Lisa!" This was the worse curse Memaw ever used. I knew something bad had happened.

"Is it Mama? Is she coming home? Lemme talk to her!"

"Lisa, you need to talk to this child," Memaw said into the phone. "She has worried her little self-sick about you."

I reached for the phone, excited to hear my mama's voice when Memaw hung up the receiver instead. Mama had ended the call. I felt sick to my stomach. My breath became fast and heavy and I burst into tears, falling to the checked yellow linoleum.

"I want my mama. She said she was coming back to get me!" Memaw reached down and picked me up, hoisting me to her chest, just like I had seen her do Debbie so many times. I buried my wet face in her shoulder and cried until I thought I was going to be sick. She carried me down the hall and into the bedroom, then fetched a cold damp cloth from the bathroom to wipe my puffy face. I had almost cried myself to sleep when I asked the final question.

"Is my mama ever coming back?"

"Maybe soon, baby. Maybe soon."

Chapter 6

One August night, nearly three months since I had seen my mama, I was standing in a chair helping Memaw wash dishes at the kitchen sink when I heard familiar music blaring from a car radio. We looked at each other for a moment, then I jumped down from the chair and ran to the carport door. The black Trans-Am was there, and two small children ran up to me.

"Scotty! Niki!" I exclaimed, squeezing so tightly I felt like I would cut off their circulation.

At that moment, Mama walked around the corner.

"Mama!" I released my death grip on Scotty and Niki and ran to her. I wrapped myself around her legs.

"Now get off of me so I can go inside," she said, pushing me away from her. "It's hot out here."

Once she got inside, her demeanor changed. "Memaw, we sure did miss you while we were gone," she said in the high-pitched, southern saccharine tone she used when she was trying her best to win someone over after she had done something wrong.

"You got a lotta' nerve, child," Memaw said. "Walkin' in here like you hadn't done a thing wrong. Where in the world have you been? You had me worried to death. And your poor child—"

"I can understand why that damned mother of mine never has a kind thing to say about me," Mama interrupted. "She hates the ground I walk on… but you?"

"Jackie hasn't said a word about you, and I'm not insinuating anything bad about you either, it's just the things you do," Memaw said, giving in to avoid a fuss. "You're back now and that's all that matters, I reckon."

I was still angry at Mama for leaving, and wished Memaw would try harder to get some answers out of her, since I knew she would never answer to me. A huge lump rose in my throat, but I knew better than to cry. Instead, I hunched in the recliner next to Memaw, my muscles tight as I watched Mama sit down on the blue couch across the room.

"Aren't you gonna come over here and give your mama some love, Pangie Bear?" she said, finally speaking to me and holding out her arms for a hug.

It always confused me when Mama was affectionate all of a sudden. It might be genuine, or it might be a warning signal for something else, a bad mood about to explode. Just like the tears she used to talk her way out of bad situations, her love turned on and off like a light switch. However, despite the way she had shrugged me off under the carport, I ran to her now, to the voice that for the moment sounded as sweet as an angel singing. I threw myself into her lap, wrapping my arms around her neck and placing my cheek firmly against her cheek, feeling her warm soft skin. All of my anger and disappointment vanished in an instant.

"I'm glad you're home, Mama. I missed you so much." I wanted to beg her never to go away again, but I had learned, even in one of her rare good moods, not to push my luck.

"Go see what your brother and sister are up to," she said, pushing me off her lap.

Scotty and Niki were already playing outside on Memaw's front lawn in the twilight. We laughed as we wrestled and tumbled on the soft grass. I was so happy that we were back together again, but it felt different now for some reason. I had been accustomed to taking care of them for Mama, but they'd lived without me for three months. They had grown a lot since I had last seen them and both were very tan. It was strange to see how tall they'd grown, how strong Niki was. Did they even need me anymore?

"Where did y'all go?" I asked.

"Mama got married again and we had a black daddy," Scotty said. "His name was Ray. We lived with him in Florida, real close to the beach too!"

I lay there on the ground, watching the lightening bugs fly around me, trying to absorb the words I had just heard. It wasn't surprising to me that Mama had found a new man; I was used to seeing her with all kinds of different men. But thinking about a new daddy made me remember our last daddy, and how he'd treated me.

"Does that mean Jerry Bramble's not our daddy anymore?" I asked.

"I don't know," Scotty said. "Mama and Ray got in a big fight so we came back here."

My heart clenched and I thought about Jerry's pet snake, Boey. I hoped Scotty was wrong, that Jerry would stay away forever and that our new daddy, Ray, would be nice. I'd rather have a stranger, no matter how bad, than have to face Jerry again.

"I'm glad you're home, brother," I whispered, squeezing Scotty again. Even though he looked a little different, he was still my brother. We could fight each other as hard as any two siblings, but we also looked out for each other. When there wasn't enough food, I made sure he got to eat and I would do without, and after Mama had been rough with me, he always snuck behind her back to give me hugs. At the end of the day, I wanted to protect him and his presence always comforted me.

When we went to bed that night, I made a pallet in the living room for the three of us to sleep on. While I tried to fall asleep, I overheard a conversation between Granny and Mama in the kitchen.

"Well, Lisa, where are you planning to stay?"

"I thought we could just stay here at your house until I find a job," Mama said. "Jerry and I are gonna look for a new house."

I felt like I was going to throw up. My heart raced and my palms began to sweat. Why couldn't we just keep our new black daddy from Florida? Why couldn't we live at Memaw's house? Why did we *ever* have to see Jerry again?

I listened for Memaw to speak. Jerry had flown into rages in front of her before, even going so far as to break some items in her house. I had wondered, even as a child, if Memaw ever suspected any of the other things he did to me behind closed doors. I hoped she would try to talk Mama out of going back to him.

But instead I heard her say, "That's fine, Lisa. Y'all are always welcome here."

Chapter 7

That fall, I was supposed to start first grade. But Mama had ignored all of Granny Jack's requests to get me enrolled, claiming that she had enough to do without worrying about me.

"You need to get off your dead-beat ass and get this child signed up for school," I heard Granny Jack say from the kitchen. "Lord knows we don't need her turning out like your sorry ass!"

"If you want her in school, you're gonna have to deal with her," Mama responded.

"They are gonna take her away from you if you don't get your shit together and start taking care of her, Lisa Ann." Granny Jack was really angry at Mama when she used both names. "I don't want her gettin' put into no damn orphanage. Hell, kids die in them places."

Granny's words scared me. I had heard Granny Jack and Paw talking about trying to keep me out of an orphanage on multiple occasions and not long after my mom dumped me at Memaw's.

"The woman from the state said they are gonna take her away and put her in foster care," Paw said. "We've got to do something, Jackie. We can't just turn her over to strangers."

I didn't know what was about to happen, but I made my mind up right then, I would *never* go to an orphanage. A car door slammed, a familiar sound, and Lisa drove away down the gravel drive. Granny Jack came back in the house.

"Are you hungry? Granny will fix you something to eat, then we will go and meet with a nice man."

On the way Granny did most of the talking, explaining to me that my mom didn't really want me. She told me that, if I told the judge the right things, I could live with her and Paw forever. In fact, I could even draw a check for a thousand dollars a month if I was in their legal care, and that money could be used for my clothes and school supplies. But I needed to tell him that I wanted to stay with them and not my mama. At the time, I was confused and nervous. I loved my Mama and wanted to stay with her.

Granny Jack pointed out that, if I didn't tell the judge that I wanted to live with her and Paw, that I would be taken away from them and have to live with strangers or even be put in an orphanage.

What if Mama finds out I said I didn't want to live with her? Would she ever even want to see me again? I thought wildly as we pulled in front of a tall white courthouse. I was silent as we got out of the car and began walking up the sidewalk that led to the entrance of the building.

Granny tried to convince me one more time.

"If you just tell the judge you want to live with me and Paw, we will go shopping right after and get you new Barbies and that Barbie car you wanted, and we will never have to talk about this again," Granny said.

When we left the courthouse, I was legally adopted. My grandparents were now my parents. I had mixed feelings about this. Granny could be as violent and unpredictable as Mama sometimes, which scared me. I never knew when she would fly off the handle. But at their house, I always had enough to eat and I knew I had a safe bed to sleep in. The part I liked the most was that I got their last name, Reed, instead of having to live with the last name 'Leech,' which had already caused me a lot of torment.

The next day we drove the three miles to Chickasaw Academy. This was where my aunt Kim, Granny Jack's youngest daughter, was in tenth grade. I had been in the gymnasium before to see Kim cheer, but had never been in the long, red-brick schoolhouse itself. While Granny talked to the secretary and the principal in the front office, I sat in a chair looking down the long hallway and feeling excited. From where I sat, I could hear Granny Jack explaining that my mother didn't take care of me, so she was stuck with having to enroll me in school. The secretary told her how much the tuition was but said that Granny would get a price break because Kim was already enrolled there.

"I don't care how much it cost," Granny Jack said. "I'm not gonna have anybody in my house goin' to that public school in Okolona with a bunch of damn niggers and gays."

I didn't understand what the word 'gay' meant, but I had a nebulous sense that the 'N word' was derogatory. I also didn't like that Granny Jack didn't want me to be friends with black people. The black people who lived in the projects had always been much nicer to me than any of the white people who lived in Okolona, especially the upper-class whites who would play with me when their parents were not around but would never invite me to birthday parties. I realized then that, if I went to Chickasaw

Academy, I'd be leaving behind all my friends from the projects in Okolona. Worse, I would be leaving behind Renee.

But all that went out of my head when Granny Jack walked out of the office.

"Let's go shopping," she said. "We're gonna have you lookin' like the best dressed young'un in the whole school." In addition to the Barbies she promised, she bought me brand new school clothes and supplies for me, and even got me a special square metal lunch box with my favorite Muppet, Miss Piggy, on it.

I liked going to Chickasaw Academy. My first-grade teacher, Mrs. James, was kind and interesting and, just like in kindergarten, I quickly became teacher's pet by volunteering to do chores and read aloud during our reading groups. I never received praise or accolades at home, so I wanted my teachers and my peers to see that I was smart, to respect me. In a way, I felt like it made up for fact that I didn't have consistent parents or a stable living environment. I felt bad that my family lived in the projects, but when I was the fastest reader or the best speller, I felt successful and proud, like there was one area of my life I had control over.

Each day, I was the first one out at recess, climbing directly to the top of the tall dome-shaped monkey bars that looked like a spaceship. There I sat, taking in the view of the dirt playground, lined with large pine trees as far as I could see. And at the end of almost every school day, I went home to stay with Granny Jack and Paw, who lived closer to Chickasaw Academy. Their beautiful cedar-sided house, on ten acres of rolling countryside, was another safe space for me, as long as I could avoid Granny Jack's temper. I had my own bedroom, down the hall from their daughter Kim's bedroom, and a red-and-white striped swing set to play on.

On the weekends, I stayed with Memaw or Mama and Jerry. When I stayed at Memaw's, I got to ride bikes and play Barbies with Renee. When I stayed in the projects with Mama and Jerry, I got to catch lightning bugs with my brother and sister. It was nice to have a rhythm to my life again, and to be able to – mostly – avoid Jerry, who was working during the weeks or getting high with his friend Sammy on the weekends.

But everything changed the summer after first grade, when Mama announced that she and Jerry had found a house to move into – and that I'd be coming along.

Chapter 8

The new place was about thirty minutes outside of Okolona and, as we made our way down the gravel drive with all our things, I found myself looking for landmarks I could identify in case I needed to get away. The house was surrounded by pines and oaks and, nearby there was a pond full of tadpoles. The only other thing in sight was a small country church that shared the same gravel drive.

The house itself sat up on blocks and looked like it was leaning to one side. The white paint had faded to beige and the wood trim was rotted around the entire house. On the porch, there were three plastic lawn chairs and a blue plastic milk crate that had been turned upside down to hold an ashtray.

Inside, it was small, with old wood floors that creaked every time anyone took a step. We didn't have a real kitchen table, just two old sawhorses and a piece of plywood that we'd draped a tablecloth over. I shared a pallet with Scotty and Niki again, in the bedroom across from Jerry and Mama. Out our bedroom window, I could see the church in the distance. I was intrigued by the people I saw coming and going from the church on Sundays, all smiling. I had been to the Church of Christ a few times with Memaw, and remembered how there was a moment in the service where the children got to hear a special story just for them, and afterwards were given candy.

One morning I woke to the sound of Jerry getting ready for work. I stayed on the pallet pretending I was asleep until I heard him leave, then went to the kitchen to fix myself some cereal. There was hardly any milk left so I saved it for my brother and sister and ate a piece of loaf bread instead. Then, as the sun rose, I snuck out of the house to explore.

I tried to peer into the church's stained glass windows but I couldn't see in. I made my way to the front of the church and up the concrete steps and I placed my hand on the curvy door handle. To my surprise, it opened. After quickly checking to ensure no one was around, I crept inside and gently closed the door behind me.

"Hello," I called.

No one answered so I ventured in. The carpet was deep red and its softness felt good to my bare feet. I walked about halfway down the center aisle and sat down on one of the wooden pews. I stared around me – at the large wooden cross hanging behind the pulpit, the white doves in the stained glass. Everything was so peaceful.

I thought about a rhyme I'd learned in school and wove my fingers together with the bottom of my palms touching. Raising my two index fingers together to form a point, I then spread my hands open wiggling all my fingers.

"This is the church, this is the steeple. Open the doors and see all the people. Close the doors and let them pray. Open the doors and they have all gone away."

Before too long, I heard Scotty calling my name outside of the church. I didn't want anyone to know I had found a way in, so I ran out the front door and back toward the house where Scotty was. We played together and I picked a bouquet of wildflowers from the field to surprise Mama. If I did something nice for her, I thought she might be in a good mood and we could go and buy us groceries.

When I got home, I eased into Mama's bedroom and crept to the side of her bed. I leaned down and kissed her pale, freckled cheek and whispered in her ear.

"Mama… are you awake? I have a surprise for you." I gave her a gentle nudge as she began to move around in the bed. "I brought you flowers, Mama. I cut them all by myself."

"What in hell are you waking me up for?" she said, tossing the flowers on the bedside table. "Get the hell outta here and go get your brother and sister some breakfast. And don't bother me again while I am tryin' to sleep."

After breakfast, Scotty and I went down to the pond. We played in the water, daring each other to see how far we could wade, laughing as small fish swam near our feet. In that moment I felt free. There was nothing in sight but the clear blue sky, big trees, and the sparkling water. Between the pond and the church, I thought perhaps I had found my sanctuary in this new place.

Maybe I could be safe here.

"Daddy Jerry is home from work," Scotty announced suddenly, pointing at the truck pulling into our drive. "We gotta go, sis."

He led the way back to the house, chopping at the tall grass with a stick he picked up. I lagged behind, nervous about seeing Jerry again. I tried to convince Scotty to climb the big tree in the front yard, but he was too tired and hungry. I climbed it alone, doing anything to avoid going inside. Even while Jerry called my name, I hid up there, watching the lightning bugs until they were completely faded out of sight and wishing I could fly away like one of them.

"Where have you been?" Jerry yelled when I finally walked into the living room.

I stared at him like I was looking right through him. I felt proud that I had tricked him and had managed to keep my new hiding spot a secret. Keeping secrets from him always made me feel like I was winning the game he created.

"If you can't speak to me then you don't get supper! Is that clear?"

"I'm not hungry anyway," I retorted.

That night, I lay on the pallet cuddling Niki until she was fast asleep. It wasn't long before I heard Jerry walking down the hall and saw his tall silhouette in the door.

"Princesses like you don't sleep on the floor," he said sarcastically. "You're sleeping in the bed with me tonight."

I began to cry, refusing to get up off the pallet. But, with one hard jerk of my arm, Jerry had me on my feet. He led me across the hall to the bedroom where Mama lay asleep on one side, passed out from sleeping pills. I began to shake, breathing so hard it felt like the only sound in the world. He laid me on the bed, then lay down on top of me.

I kept my face turned away, focusing on the moon shining through the curtain-less window and the dead flowers still lying on the nightstand. I imagined the flowers were alive in a beautiful open field, and that I was there, running freely among the flowers, or swimming in the pond again, the mud squishing between my toes. When Jerry finally pushed away from me, I continued to lie there, my body stiff and my face streaked from silent tears. I imagined finding a gun, like the one Memaw kept under her pillow, and shooting him with it, or bashing his head in with a hammer.

I don't remember falling asleep but the next morning I woke to the harsh sound of his voice.

"Look at what you have done!" he screamed on his way out the door. "You get in that bathroom and clean your mess up!"

There was blood staining the bed sheets and splotched on the tile around the toilet. I got a rag and cleaned up around the toilet, then tried to clean the sheets the same way, but the blood kept spreading around, soaking through the material. I was so ashamed that I'd made a mess. Was I a bad person? Was this my fault? It seemed like it was, because when Mama woke up, she yelled at me for it too.

It was hard for me to pee, sit, or even walk for a few days. Eventually Mama took me to Dr. Shoemaker, telling him I had a UTI. Without examining me, he prescribed me medication and then Mama took me to Memaw's house. As we pulled in the drive, she leaned over the console grabbed my shirt, and pulled me toward her. Putting her forehead right against mine, she stared directly into my eyes without blinking.

"You ruin everything, you little wench!" she said through clenched teeth, before taking me inside to Memaw.

That was the last time I ever had to share a house with Jerry Bramble. It was also the last time I saw Mama for nearly a year.

The Body: 2

The coroner pulled in directly after I arrived. The Jones County Morgue was the place they took indigent or unidentified people and the coroner seemed to be in a rush, fumbling through her keys trying to find the right one for the lock on the dirty metal door. Then she took me into a concrete block room that was hardly large enough to accommodate the cold metal gurney where Lisa's body lay. The white body bag was unzipped only enough that her head and face were exposed.

It was her. Same long hair, dyed now to cover the grey. Same deep-set eyes. I touched her face, feeling the coolness of her scalp and forehead, before being overcome with a desire to see her hands.

"Why do you want to see her hands?" the coroner asked.

I didn't know why. It just felt important that I touch her hands again one last time. "Can I have a moment alone?" I asked instead of answering her question.

The coroner hurriedly unzipped the bag down to Lisa's waist. She roughly plopped her left arm out from the bag and let it hang off the side of the table. "I'm running behind, but I can give you a few minutes," she said gruffly.

A moment later, I was alone with Lisa. I walked down the side of the gurney to where her hand was dangling. I examined her short, rigid fingers. Her fingernails were bitten to the quick just like always. She was wearing a wedding ring I didn't recognize. I studied the homemade cross tattoo on her wrist and the mottling on her arm where her flesh had already started the process of decomposition.

Mothers are often identified with their soft, kind hands. Braiding their daughters' hair in the morning before school, making their son his favorite meal on his birthday, or just rubbing a child's shoulders to lull them to sleep after a nightmare. But my biggest association with my mother's hands was the smell of smoke, the bright flame of fire.

Lisa smoked incessantly, two or three packs a day until her hair and skin always smelled. She also loved fire. By her own account, she had burned down houses before, sometimes in an act of pleasure, sometimes one of revenge. I found it more than a little ironic that, when they'd found her body, there was a burn circle in the carpet where she'd dropped her cigarette. In death, she hadn't managed to do what she loved to do in life.

But the most painful memory of Lisa's hands was this: if she was in a particularly bad mood, she would make me sit next to her while she smoked, squeezing my arm with one hand. With the other, she'd lower the cigarette over the skin of my wrist, holding it there just above the surface until the lit cherry of the cigarette heated my skin red-hot and I squirmed away from it. The entire time, she'd look back and forth between my arm and my face, an expression of hateful fascination, chanting "You ruined my life, you little wench; see what you've done!"

She was always careful not to leave a mark, a shiny burn scar. When I got old enough to reflect on it, I wondered if that was because it would have been noticed by someone else, or because she knew that it would kill the nerves – that burning me this way would hurt worse.

The most painful part was that I never saw her do anything like this with anyone else. I didn't understand why I, out of all her kids, should be the sole recipient of her violence and disgust. What had I done to earn her hatred?

Chapter 9

In second grade, something happened that would change my life. I was voted a homecoming maid. For the ceremony, Granny Jack rented a long powder-blue chiffon gown with white lace down the front. While we still had the dress, Granny Jack decided to enter me in the school beauty review, a popular beauty contest that most girls my age entered. I had seen Kim and other friends competing in similar reviews, and I was excited to get on stage myself. The elementary students worked with older students on walking, turning on stage, and other pageant skills. At home, I practiced relentlessly and, when the day came, I realized I loved it. Even better, I won queen in my division. When that crown was placed on my head, it was the first time I could remember having something that I felt no one could take away. Even Mama's snide remark when she found out – "You must have been the only one competing" – couldn't take away my joy.

Granny Jack, loving the attention my win brought her, began to search for other pageants to enter me in. She even got a couple different business owners to sponsor the pageants that I was in, so getting me new clothes didn't cost anything. Sometimes there was even money left over. For a couple years, it seemed like I competed in pageants almost every weekend, calling Memaw excitedly when I won to tell her about my prizes and crowns.

By the time summer came I had an entire shelf of crowns and trophies lining one entire wall in my bedroom. I had even competed in a national competition, performing the Dolly Parton song *9 to 5*. When I won the talent competition, I caught the interest of a local vocal coach.

Pete Doles was well known in Tupelo for his role in bringing pageant girls to top rankings in competitions. He was in his early 40s, with olive skin, broad shoulders, and a deep whiskey voice. I thought of him as a gentle giant. Granny Jack scheduled my first singing lesson with Pete before we even left the pageant. It wasn't long until I was spending a lot of time with Pete and his wife, Rosa, at their small house in Tupelo.

I typically spent two or three days with them when I went for a voice lesson, often because no one showed up to get me. If they minded this imposition, they were good at hiding it. Rosa didn't speak English very well, but she let me know I was loved and safe in other ways, by cooking for me, making sure I had clean clothes while I was at their house, and sitting with me on the couch while I waited for my ride. When other students came, I sat on the floor in the back of the room just to listen to them sing. Pete played the piano like no one I'd ever heard, pounding the keys hard without even glancing at the music.

Pete could also be an intimidating person. He never minced words when giving feedback to his students, whether they sounded good or horrible. Many times I heard him matter-of-factly tell a crying student, "Dry it up! Your mama ain't payin' me all this money for you to sit here and cry!" For some reason, though, I was never intimidated by him. I wanted to do everything perfect for him and Rosa.

One of the songs Pete taught me was *I Enjoy Being a Girl* from the musical *Flower Drum Song*, which I sang at several competitions.

"Come sit right here next to me," he said, patting a spot next to him on the piano bench. Then he leaned over to look me straight in the face while he played the tune perfectly on the piano. He always kept a cup of coffee with whiskey in it sitting on top of the piano and I found the smell of the coffee and whiskey on his breath comforting.

"I enjoy being a girl," he sang, making me giggle at the lyrics belted out in his strong, raspy voice.

"And I enjoy seeing my girls sing," Rosa said, watching us with a smile.

The most important song Pete taught me was *Don't Cry Out Loud*, the Melissa Manchester hit. I couldn't hit the higher notes toward the end of the song, but Pete rewrote the notes so that they weren't so high for me and we sang it every week.

When I sang the lyrics, I felt like Pete had somehow seen directly into my soul. Did he know that my mama hit me when I cried, and that Granny Jack had forbidden crying in her house? At the time, I didn't think so, but later in life I wondered if he could tell what I was going through at the time, doing his best to help me.

"Music can carry you through anything, baby, and it will never leave you," he once told me. For the next two years Pete and Rosa didn't leave me, either.

Chapter 10

Even though I was still at Chickasaw, I still got to see Renee on the weekends and spent most of my summers with her for the next couple of years. When Renee's dad was on leave for Army drill during the weekends, her mom would leave us alone to babysit her brother for the entire weekend. We were given strict instructions not to answer the phone, and especially *never* tell anyone that she was gone.

To entertain ourselves while they were gone, we made up games to entertain her brother, Steadman. We banged out tunes on her toy piano, rearranging the words to Jerry Lee Lewis songs, singing *Great Balls of Boogers* instead of *Great Balls of Fire.* With their video camera, we made our own fake weight-loss commercials, stuffing her dad's clothes with pillows then pulling all the pillows out, tossing them to the side, and saying "This was me then, and this is me now." We sang and danced around the house to songs like *A Boy Named Sue* and *Does Your Chewing Gum Lose Its Flavor?* and made banana boats by splitting a banana in half-long ways and piling it with chocolate bars and marshmallows, placing it in the oven until everything was bubbly.

By the end of fourth grade, rumors were spreading that Renee's mom was having an affair with a black man, a big taboo in 1985 when Okolona still had an active Ku Klux Klan. We had wondered where she was going on the weekends Renee's dad was away, but we didn't hear the rumors until we were swimming at the Wilson Park pool during the summer. Most of our Wilson Park friends came from wealthier homes than the people we were used to seeing in Renee's neighborhood. These kids played with us at the park and in the swimming pool, but when their parents arrived to pick them up, they ignored us. It was like we suddenly became invisible.

Eventually, the kids began to make jokes about Renee's mother – and mine. "Looks like both of you have white-trash, nigger-lovin' mamas now," said Beth, the daughter of a prominent political figure in Okolona.

When Renee began to cry, I became furious at our tormenters. Immediately I started spilling everything I had ever heard about their families from Granny Jack gossiping with her cousin.

"Your mama sleeps with one of the deacons at church," I pointed out to one girl. I turned to another girl. "And your mama and daddy traded sex with their friends."

It made me mad that I didn't have more gossip to use as ammunition. It was near impossible to defend our mothers, especially mine. Renee and I walked home in silence.

"No wonder our mamas are such good friends," I said, trying to cheer her up. "They both have the same taste in men. Hell, me and you both probably got a little African blood running through our veins. That's probably why we can dance better than any white bitch around us!" I started dancing down the street.

Renee finally let out a chuckle through her tears and I felt like I had fixed things for her.

But the following week we woke to Renee's mother yelling at us in the middle of the night.

"Get out of bed!" she shrieked. Through the blinds, I could see a bright light in the front yard. There were two wooden crosses burning in the front yard right next to the driveway where Sue's Suzuki Jeep sat, its ragtop painted in tar and feathers. Renee and I got Steadman from his bed and held him tightly between us while we watched the firemen extinguish the blaze that had spread around the yard.

Not long after the burning of the crosses we were riding our mopeds in her yard, doing figure eights between the pear trees that still stood slightly burned by the fire. Two boys from the small brick house next door came out. We had never liked them; they were bullies who made fun of us, challenging us to arm wrestling competitions and then mocking us when we lost. On this day, they started throwing rocks at us while calling us names and making fun of our mothers.

"Nigger lovers!"

"Whores!"

A large rock went into the spokes of Renee's wheel, making her fall over. I stopped my moped and jumped off, running to see if Renee was okay. When I saw that she was, I ran across the yard, leaping on top of the first boy I could get to. I tackled him to the ground, cursing him like a sailor during the process.

"You little fucker!" I screamed, punching him as hard as I could with my knee planted in his groin. "Your mama is a fucking whore! If you ever say another word to me or Renee, I will stab you through the throat with a tree branch!"

Their mom came out of the house and started cursing at Renee and me.

"Get off them, you little heathens!" she yelled. "I'm going to tell your father, Renee!"

I was so engulfed with anger that I just wouldn't give up until the boy's mother pulled me off and slung me out of the way.

"You better be scared to go to sleep," I screamed, walking backwards to Renee's house so I could maintain a direct stare at the boy. "You better be glad you didn't hurt Renee, you damn punk."

Renee and I had already been nearly inseparable, but sharing these experiences created a deeper bond between us. I had never been afraid to die before, but that night of the burning crosses, I remember a tremendous fear that they would set the house on fire, burning us alive. I wanted Renee to feel my full commitment and loyalty to her, to know that I had her back and to feel like she had mine, so the next day we pricked our fingers with a safety pin until our blood flowed, and then we pressed our fingertips together tightly. We vowed to be sisters that no one could ever separate.

After this, I wanted to tell Renee about what Jerry had done to me.

"I have something to tell you," I said one weekend when we'd been left alone. "It's something I never told anyone else." Before I could speak, though, visions of Jerry engulfed my thoughts. He'd threatened to feed me to Boey if I ever told anyone. I started crying.

"Why are you crying, Angie?" she asked. In all the time we'd been together, through teasing and threats, she'd never seen me cry before.

"I can't tell you," I decided.

"Please, you can trust me," she pleaded as I remained silent. "Did someone hurt you? I'll kill them."

That scared me so much that I turned the radio on as loud as it would go, and started dancing in the living room. She kept asking me to talk to her, and I just shook my head and danced until she joined me. Within a few minutes, we had both forgotten what had just happened.

Just a few weeks before fifth grade was going to start, it was announced that Chickasaw Academy would be closing. Since it was the most stable thing I had in my life so far, I was crushed to lose my teachers and my friends. But Renee and I both hoped this meant we could spend more time together. We were riding double on her moped, heading back into town from having a picnic on one of our favorite trails, when we heard a car slowing and calling for Renee out of the window. It was her dad.

"Renee, come home right now. We have to leave."

We followed him back to the house where he already had bags packed for her and Steadman. They were leaving Okolona, and Sue, behind. Renee screamed and cried until she threw up in the driveway. We embraced each other so tightly we had to be forced apart. Within thirty minutes, they were gone.

As I watched the pale blue sedan fade out of sight, I walked to a large tree in the yard and sat down on the ground under it. My chest hurt. I don't remember how long I sat there but I knew it would be years before I would see Renee again.

Chapter 11

The summer I was ten, Memaw took me to First Baptist for Vacation Bible School. Even though I had been drawn to the country church near the little white house, the only times I had attended a church service were Memaw's occasional visits to Wednesday night services at the Church of God and an occasional Sunday morning service. Neither my mama nor Granny Jack ever took me. Granny Jack had always blamed God for her sister Deb being born with cerebral palsy. "If there *is* a God, He's an awful cruel one," she would say, a comment that bothered me since everyone else I knew in Mississippi said you'd go straight to hell if you didn't believe in God.

But some of my school friends went to First Baptist and I had always seen them playing fun games outside when I rode past on my bike. I thought I might like to try going to church.

By the end of the week of VBS, I decided I wanted to be baptized. I was full of excitement to join the church and be a real part of it, so I went to talk to my Sunday school teacher. Miss Nancy was an attractive, petite woman with silver hair who always dressed in the best clothes – skirt suits or dresses with wide belts and accessories to match.

When I asked her about it, she took a long look at me, wearing a tee shirt and jean shorts.

"Sweetie, if you want to be baptized and keep coming to church," she said in a snobby Southern drawl, "you are gonna have to find some better clothes to wear. Don't you know that you need to wear dresses on Sunday?"

Her words stuck with me longer than anything else I learned in VBS. I was so embarrassed and angry that I considered kicking her in the leg. Instead, I walked briskly out of the church, climbed on my bike and rode as fast as I could down the Main Street sidewalk.

At this moment I believed that my Granny Jack was right. I knew that if God was as good as everyone said, he would never let anyone who proclaimed to be a Christian look down on others like that.

"Fuck you!" I cursed up to the sky. "You are a mean son of a bitch and I hate you!" It was God's fault that I couldn't go to my old school, that Renee had left, that I didn't have a daddy and Mama didn't want me. On top of all of this, I was resentful that my voice had changed and I had stopped winning talent competitions at pageants.

I didn't realize why I was losing talent competitions until I heard myself on a recorded performance one day singing *Diamonds Are a Girl's Best Friend*. I had gone from being a decent singer to way off key, with absolutely dreadful tone. But these pageants were the only consistently good thing in my life, and I was determined not to let that stop me. I loved performing and I clung to the proud expression on Pete's face every time he looked at me while beating out notes on the piano, every time I won a competition singing the songs he taught me.

But Pete was sick. He couldn't train me anymore. He had no energy; sometimes the breath that previously carried him through hours on end singing could hardly last him through one song. His arms and torso that were once stout and muscular began to shrink. And then one weekend he didn't show up for the pageant, or the one the weekend after.

No one would tell me what was wrong with him, when he was going to get better. I didn't understand why he had stopped showing up.

I needed to find a new talent and an outlet for my anger and loss. I had always been intrigued with Shari Lewis and her sock puppet, Lamb Chop, but I had never once considered ventriloquism as talent until I noticed a female ventriloquist at a pageant. She was about eight years older than me, nearing the end of her competition years, and her singing abilities were almost as poor as mine. However, she won nearly every time because she was singing through a puppet without moving her mouth.

She's winning talent because she isn't moving her mouth? I was instantly intrigued. After just a few days of practicing singing without moving my lips in front of a mirror, I announced to my grandmother that I would start being a ventriloquist.

"Granny, I may sing bad, but I'm a ventriloquist. Shari Lewis has her own television show and Amy wins every talent competition she enters."

She brushed me off telling me that ventriloquism was a very hard thing and took a 'special kind of talent.' I followed her as she turned and walked away from me.

"Look at me," I pleaded as she finally turned around to appease me. "Please, I can really do this."

67

As she watched me speak and sing without moving my lips, her eyes grew in amazement. But she remained skeptical that I could put everything together.

"That's real good, but that's not all there is to it. It's a lot different when you have a puppet on your arm," she said. "It takes a lot of coordination. You have to be smart and talented to pull everything together. You just couldn't do it."

This made me feel more determined than ever. I went straight to Paw and asked him if I could have an old sock. With a black magic marker, I drew eyes and a mouth, and added a tongue with a red marker. I spent the next two days placing the sock puppet on my hand and practicing in the mirror. One of my favorite movies was *The Wizard of Oz,* so I learned to sing *Follow the Yellow Brick Road.*

After the second day of practice, I carefully positioned the sock puppet on my hand and stood in the living room to perform for Granny Jack. She didn't compliment me, but I could tell that she was convinced and a couple weeks later she bought me a monkey arm puppet. He had chocolate brown fur, a tan face, and large eyes. I named him Andy and spent hours sitting in front of the long mirror that hung on the wall next to my closet, practicing with him.

In absence of Renee, of Pete, of other people I could trust, Andy became my best friend. When kids at school made fun of me for not having regular parents or called my mom a whore... when church-ladies like Miss Nancy looked down on me... when Granny Jack screamed at me and hit me... it was Andy I turned to. If someone hurt me, it was Andy who cursed and called them names on my behalf.

I was able to divert the tension I felt by practicing with Andy. For the first time, I was able to express my feelings aloud, but the words weren't coming from me; they were coming from him. Somehow that fact made it okay to express the anger I felt towards Granny or Mama, instead of feeling guilty or like I owed them my love. He was only a simple puppet, but he was also the only thing that I had complete control over, the only thing to defend and comfort me.

Not long after I got Andy, Granny Jack had a big loss at the casino. The next day, the house was almost silent. Paw, who had just come home from the hospital after a heart attack, tried to lighten the mood and create some normalcy in the house by watching her favorite TV shows and making light-hearted jokes for most of the morning. But it was a simple request that set her off.

"Baby, will you fix me a glass of tea?" Paw asked.

She fixed him a full glass of ice tea and, as he thanked her, she flung the glass of tea across the room. The glass hit Paw in the head, breaking his skin. I saw blood trickle down the side of his face. Furious, Paw got up out of his recliner in one swift motion and put his foot through the glass-and-wicker coffee table. More glass flew onto the floor, and Granny Jack attacked him. I was afraid that Paw might have another heart attack as he fought Granny Jack off him. I tried to come to his rescue, but Granny Jack shoved me to the ground.

"Go to your damn room or you'll be next!" she snarled.

I spent the rest of the day in my room with Andy, trying to abide by Granny Jack's steadfast rule of 'no crying.' I wrapped Andy's arms around my neck, and velcroed his hands together like he was hugging me.

"Don't cry. Do you see me crying?" he told me, moving his head to look at me. "Don't even blink if she comes in here. Just look at her like I'm looking at you. I'll cuss her out if she hits you!"

I actually began to laugh at Andy and at myself for sitting in the floor talking to a puppet. I heard Granny coming down the hall and when Andy turned his head toward the door and said, "Fuck you, you munchkin ass bitch!" I laughed even harder. The thought of a monkey saying that made me giggle so hard that Granny Jack flung my door open to see why I was laughing. She hadn't heard what he said, but the look of confusion on her face as she saw me sitting in the floor laughing with my puppet was just as entertaining to me as Andy himself.

Chapter 12

When I was eleven years old, I won Overall Supreme Queen in a summer pageant in Jackson, Tennessee – my first big win on a national level. I now had two puppets, Andy and a girl monkey named Amy. As I came off of the stage from the talent portion with my puppets, I was greeted by the most beautiful little girl, with sandy blonde hair, big blue eyes, and the best tan I'd ever seen on a five-year-old.

"I wanna see that monkey talk again," she said, grabbing at Andy. "Make him talk for me!"

She was so cute it was not hard to follow through with her request. I made Andy ask, "What's your name, little girl?"

"Chelsea Hawwison," she replied. The lisp of her 'r's made her even cuter.

As I stood entertaining Chelsea, her mother appeared, apologizing for the interruption of her young daughter.

"It's no problem," I assured her as we walked toward the back of the ballroom. Chelsea was still in awe of the monkeys so I placed one of them on her arm so that she could see how it worked. She ran off to show her big sister Jesse, a nine-year-old with strawberry blonde hair and blue eyes who was the reigning queen from the year before. I showed them both how to make the puppets move and talk, and we formed an immediate bond.

For the next two days of competition, Chelsea and Jesse stayed as close to me as they possibly could. Chelsea sat in my lap every time I sat down and liked for me to pick her up and carry her around the rest of the time. Jesse told me I had a funny accent, but she loved hearing me talk.

By the time the competition ended, I had learned a lot about the Harrison family. Jan, their mother, had a flawless complexion and beautiful reddish blonde hair that was always perfectly cut. An artist who worked from home, she was sweet and jolly, and very talented at designing pageant gowns. Their father, Bill, was tall and tan, with a perfect circle of dark brown hair around his balding head. He worked for the federal government, and sold used cars and jewelry as a hobby. Together Jan and Bill were the sweetest and most attentive parents I had ever seen at this point in my life. I loved the way their eyes lit up every time they glanced at their girls.

At eleven years old, I was already doing my own hair and makeup at pageants, but Jan must have noticed that I needed a little help. The day after I met her, she offered her assistance and made a few corrections in my eye makeup just right before I went on stage for sportswear competition. She continued to do this for the remainder of the competition. I relished the attention; it made me feel like I mattered to someone.

It didn't take Jan long to start asking questions about my life. "You are here with your grandmother?" she asked.

"Yes," I answered.

"Where are your mom and dad?"

I changed the subject, hesitant to provide any more information than I had to. I was embarrassed and worried the Harrisons might think, since my own family didn't love me, that I wasn't worth their time. I was also nervous answering questions about my family in front of Granny Jack, knowing that any little thing I said might set her off, jerking my arm or cursing me out in public.

But Jan continued to ask questions about my parents so I continued to give vague answers, trying to divert the attention to Chelsea, which was easy to do.

I had become more hesitant and guarded over the years, careful not to form bonds with people in case they left like Renee and Pete had. But there was something different about the Harrison family. I felt like they accepted me for who I was, while nurturing me to become a stronger person. Watching them interact, I could see how a true family should behave – loving, caring, and not envious of each other. I found myself strangely upset by the fact that we would all be going our separate ways after the competition was over. I thought I would probably never see them again and I didn't understand this newfound sadness about leaving complete strangers.

So, just two weeks later at The Miss Town and Country USA Pageant, when I looked down and saw Chelsea's arms wrapped around one of my legs, I was so happy. It was the first time I remember wanting to cry for joy. I ran to hug the rest of her family and Jan helped me with my hair and makeup during the entire pageant. I ended up staying in their room a couple of nights, me, Chelsea and Jesse all piled onto one bed, with Jan and Bill in the other.

As the pageant ended and we began our goodbyes, Chelsea started crying. "Can she come home with us?" she asked Jan.

Jesse and I started crying, too, and Jan turned to me and Granny Jack.

"Would you like to come home with us, Angie?" she asked. "Would that be okay with you, Jackie?"

"Sure, it's fine with me," Granny said carelessly.

I piled into their family van with nothing but the clothes I was wearing. It was strange; it was only the second time I had ever seen them, and yet I was going home with them, feeling happy and safe.

I was even more impressed with the Harrisons when I visited their house. Every morning, Bill came into the bedroom, kissed all three of us girls on the head, and told us to "take good care of Mom." I had never seen a husband and wife act so kindly and lovingly to each other before. In the evenings, after a busy day, they ate dinner together, having a family conversation and asking questions about everyone's day. They spent time getting to know me, asking about the things I liked. And at night, after Jesse and Chelsea fell asleep on my lap on the couch, I sat up with Jan, watching her paint and design pageant dresses. When I finally went to bed, Jesse or Chelsea would wake up and ask me to sleep in the middle, which I loved. Everything in their house was so easy, no fussing or yelling or hitting. Everyone respected each other, and it was entirely new to me.

After a few days, Jan asked me if I would like to stay longer. I ended up staying at their house for nearly a month. Jan periodically tried to get me to talk about my own family, but always changed the subject as soon as she felt any uneasiness from me. They treated me just like their own daughters, buying me new clothes and a few packs of Kotex when Jan noticed that I had been using homemade pads made out of toilet paper.

No matter where we went, people surrounding us thought I was a part of the family. I dragged Chelsea around like a baby doll and felt like a proud big sister to Jesse, who looked up to me and wanted to do everything just like I did. For that month, I felt like I was living life right out of a movie, like the Harrisons were my fairy god-family.

Chapter 13

When I was thirteen, I learned the truth about what had happened to Pete.

I was at Memaw's house. She called me into the kitchen on her lunch break. "Pete died, baby," she said gently. "I know you miss him and I wanted to let you know."

"He's dead? How?"

She shook her head sadly. "I heard he died of AIDS."

I walked through the woods and found a tree that I sat propped against, and I cried until I couldn't cry anymore. I had heard of AIDS and knew that there was a horrible stigma associated with it, one I didn't fully understand. But I was angry that no one had bothered to tell me earlier, to take me to visit him so I could tell him how much he meant to me. I threw every stick and rock around me, yelling at the sky, telling Pete I was sorry that I hadn't been there to help him or to say goodbye.

Later, when I got home, I pulled out some old cassette tapes that Pete had recorded for me to practice with. As I listened to the perfection of his piano playing, I could almost hear his voice singing the last phrases I ever heard him sing. I was crushed that I would never see Pete again, but at the same time I was slightly relieved that he had not abandoned me on his own. Maybe I was lovable after all.

The Harrisons did their best to show me that I was loved. For three years since I met them, there was not a birthday, Christmas, Easter, or other holiday that went by when the Harrisons did not include me as a special member of their family. They even got me the same number of Christmas gifts as their own kids, and never asked for anything in return from me. From them, I received a sense of security that I had never felt before. And I learned things I hadn't received from my own family, like basic table manners and what was appropriate to say in public. And they taught me the most valuable lesson: what it was like to be part of a functional family – in short, what true love was.

I wanted to please them more than I had ever wanted to please anyone, even my own mother. The difference was the fact that Jan and Bill were easily pleased. They thanked me for helping out around the house and praised me for taking good care of Chelsea and Jesse. I never wanted them to stop loving me.

I could hardly stand it when the time would come to leave their house, to meet Granny Jack at the halfway point in Jackson, TN. The night before I had to leave, I always cried myself to sleep in the bed next to Jesse and Chelsea. On the day of my departure, we all walked around the house heavy-hearted, with eyes full of tears.

On my fourteenth birthday, Jan and Bill arranged for me to arrive at their house. When I got there I was greeted with a birthday cake and a table filled with gifts. I had finished opening my presents when Jan looked at me with a twinkle in her eye.

"We have one more special gift for you," she said.

Bill, Jesse, and Chelsea all stood around the decorated table, as excited as Jan. She pulled out a tiny gold box from a gift bag. Inside was the most beautiful ring I had ever seen. It was an aquamarine topaz heart, surrounded by diamonds and set in white gold. I had always loved anything heart-shaped and Bill and Jan knew it. They selected this perfect ring just for me. From the moment I slid it onto my finger, I only took it off when I was playing basketball. It was a constant reminder of their love for me, and that I belonged with the Harrisons.

I had never told them much about what it was like to live at Granny's house or with Lisa and the boyfriend of the month. I felt guilty and ashamed of how chaotic and angry my life had been, nothing like their calm, loving family life. Every time I thought about talking to Jan about the abuse that I dealt with from my family, I was frozen by my mother's words, still ringing loud in my head.

"Look what you made me do… You ruined my life… You are a worthless little wench… This is all your fault!"

However, Jan and Bill both knew a lot more about my home life than I ever gave them credit for. They saw my sadness, and the indifference Granny Jack showed to me when she was around. They kept attempting to engage me in conversation about these things, but never pushed me for the answers I was unwilling to share.

Summer was approaching and Jan had already spent several months preparing me for the largest national level pageants I had ever competed in: America's Most Beautiful Girl, Town and Country USA, Dolls and Darlings, etc. With her friends, she had designed beautiful gowns for me, Jesse, and Chelsea, and spent hours coaching us on how to walk in high heels up and down stairs. We were trained to keep our heads up, our smiles bright, and never to take our eyes off the judges.

I had already won Supreme Queen at two of the pageants, earning cash and prizes, but the last one, the one that we had worked the hardest for, was "America's Most Beautiful Girls," in Memphis, TN. The night before crowning, we learned that I might be disqualified from the competition because of a vicious rumor started by my own grandmother. Granny Jack, trying to make herself look important in the pageant circuit, had begun to spread lies that I was going to win the big title that year because we knew the judges personally. That night, Jan and Bill cried with me, all of us stressed and exhausted. We had all worked so hard and it looked like it was about to be ruined.

After a sleepless night, I was overcome with emotion when the MC announced me as Supreme Queen. I stood in the crowd in shock as they waited for me to come onstage to be crowned. I didn't let go of Jan, Jesse, or Chelsea as I went on stage, and thankfully acknowledged them in my speech. My prize included a red Ford Festiva with a sign that read 'America's Most Beautiful Girl National Supreme Winner.' At fourteen, I was too young to drive, but I was excited to have my own car and hoped Granny would let me keep it.

People swarmed the stage hugging and congratulating me, but Granny Jack got angry because she wasn't getting any attention. She jerked my arm, leading me to the hallway outside the bathroom and slammed me against the wall.

"You had better pay me some attention in front of all these people!" she said, gritting her teeth. "If I see you hug those damn Harrisons one more time, I will take it all away from you!"

I thought she meant the cars, the money, and all my prizes. The material stuff was all that had ever seemed to matter to her, like the thousand-dollar check she talked about when she and Paw adopted me. I decided that, even though I liked my new red car, I didn't care what she did with my winnings. That evening, I stayed in the Harrisons hotel room again. I was careful not to take all of my makeup off because one side of my face was bruised where Granny Jack had hit me.

"Your eyes are awful dark," Jan said. "It looks like your cheek is bruised!" I had never seen such a horrified look on her face; tears formed in her blue eyes. "Has someone been hitting you?"

I had already made up a story that I could tell her, but looking into her eyes I found it impossible to lie.

"Tell me the truth, Angie," she said sternly. "You have to tell me." I could no longer hide. Tears began to stream down my face.

"You can't tell anybody," I said. "You have to promise me you will never tell anybody!"

I explained to her that Granny had a bad temper. "It's not her fault," I said. "She can't control it."

Jan slammed a makeup brush down on the bed.

"Damn it! How could she do this?" she cried. "We have to do something to stop it! I can't stand it!"

The next day, as we were all leaving the pageant, Granny surprised me, saying I was going home with her. I had planned to go home with the Harrisons and spend the summer with them just like I had for the past three years, but Granny refused. When Jesse and Chelsea begged, she only dug her heels in deeper.

"I don't want you talking to her anymore," she told them. "She is not allowed to communicate with your family ever again."

That summer, I was devastated. I was staying with Memaw most of the time again and would sneak calls to the Harrisons. Jan began to ask me what I thought about being adopted and living with them permanently. I already considered myself part of their family, like I had a real mom and dad and two wonderful little sisters, but the thought of being with them all the time made me so happy I could hardly stand it. We agreed to keep this idea a secret until they could talk to Granny about it.

But when Jan and Bill called Granny, she refused again.

"We told her that we love you, that we want you to stay with us as our own," Jan told me in a secret phone call. "But she cursed us, Angie. She is never going to give up control of you, or the money she is getting to keep you."

I was filled with resentment. I didn't care about the money, the cars, or the pageant winnings. As far as I was concerned, Granny could have it all. But even though Granny Jack continually complained about how she shouldn't have to raise me, she wouldn't let me go where there was real love.

I will never forget my last phone call from Jan.

"Angie, you know that we love you," she said, barely able to speak through her tears. "We have wanted you to be part of our family for a very long time now. But we know that can't happen. I love you so much, but I have to keep strong for Jesse and Chelsea. I hate this, Angie, but we don't want to see you get hurt and we can't handle the hurt any longer, so you are gonna have to listen to your grandmother and not call us or see us anymore."

I felt like I couldn't breathe. My heart hurt so bad that it made the rest of my body feel numb. I lay down on my bedroom floor and wailed. Granny Jack came in, infuriated that I was crying. I thought I was about to get a real Jackie Reed beating. But what she did was even worse.

"Take that damn ring off!" she said, squeezing my arm tightly and pointing to the topaz ring the Harrisons had given me. "Take it off now, goddammit!"

I saw the crazed look in her eyes and, without thinking, I did as she said, carefully removing my most prized possession from my finger. She snatched it out of my hand.

"Just like the Harrisons, you'll never see this again!"

I pulled myself from the floor and ran as fast as I could into the woods behind Granny and Paw's house. I threw rocks at trees. I kicked pinecones and tree limbs as hard as I could. I screamed and cursed at the pale blue sky. No crowns or trophies or cars could mend my shattered heart.

Chapter 14

One day I received an unexpected phone call from Mama. She had married again. Her ninth husband was a black man named Dan who was a retired Captain of the U.S. Marine Corp. I had only met him a couple of times, but he was kind and soft-spoken, and my favorite of Mama's husbands.

"I just wanted to let you know," she said excitedly, "that you are gonna have a new baby brother."

I was confused. I remembered her saying that she had undergone a hysterectomy not long after my sister Niki was born. When it suited her, though, she had a habit of making up stories about people dying or having babies, so I grilled her further.

"What are you talking about, Mama?" I asked. "You can't be pregnant."

"I am adopting a baby and it was born today. It's a little boy and he will get to come home with me day after tomorrow."

A baby? It didn't make sense. She acted like she hated me, had tossed me aside so many times. How she could possibly adopt a baby after abandoning me for so many years? I felt like I had been traded in for a younger model. Hyperventilating with anxiety, I passed out before I could ask any more questions. I woke up lying on the floor next to my bed, the phone in my hand buzzing with the dial tone. I tried calling her back but she didn't answer.

To add to my confusion and sadness, I was still aching over losing the Harrison family. We had no contact; I felt like they had died. Because of this, I was more resentful toward Granny Jack than ever. I spent most of my time now outside or alone in my bedroom. Even when she bought me a nice pair of shoes or a new outfit, I remained isolated and withdrawn. Anything she gave me, I knew, could be taken away at any time. But once I heard the news about Mama and the new baby, I found myself wanting to try again to be her daughter. I made a vow to myself that if Granny Jack ever hit me again, I was going to find Mama and move in with her.

One August morning, just a few weeks into the school year, Granny entered my room.

"Where's that denim blouse with the multi-colored buttons?" she asked.

The question was so random, I thought nothing of answering honestly. "It's at Vonda's," I told her. Vonda was one of my friends from Calhoun Academy. I often spent the night at her house during the week and sometimes kept clothes there. "I let her borrow it one day while I was staying at her house."

This was not what Granny wanted to hear. "I have to send that shirt to the goddamn cleaners," she raged, grabbing my hair, slapping and punching my face.

This was the last straw. I didn't tell her what I planned, but continued getting ready for school just as though everything was normal.

Going back with Lisa would mean leaving my school, but I was willing. I drove down the long gravel drive and headed thirty miles to Calhoun Academy just like I did every day. Once I got there, I found Vonda while keeping my sunglasses on to hide the bruise from where Granny had hit me.

"Please give this back for me," I said quietly, handing her my cheerleading uniform. "Some things have been happening at home and I have to leave. I'm going to live with my real mom."

Vonda looked at me like she was about to cry. "Take your glasses off," she said, then hugged me tight.

"When will we see you again?"

"I'm not sure," I told her. "It's a long way to where Mama lives, and I know I won't have gas money to travel that far. But I promise to come and see you as soon as I can."

I turned around and left before I started to cry. I knew I couldn't invite my friends to come and visit me at Mama's house. No one's parents would allow them to drive all the way to Caledonia, near the Air Force base where Mama lived, especially once they found out I had a black stepfather. I begged Vonda to wait a few days before she told anyone else and I drove away.

It took about two hours to get to Caledonia and my sadness at leaving my school and my friends seemed to dissipate as I envisioned the immense joy my mama would have when I told her that I was coming to live with her. I could almost feel her wrapping her arms around me and telling me how much she missed me. When I finally arrived at the tiny brown brick house, I looked around. The yard was well-kept and even though the carport smelled like cigarettes, everything was clean and tidy. Dan was particular about things like that and I thought he was good for Mama. I knocked on the door, anticipating Mama's face.

"What in the hell are you doing here?" she asked as she glared at me from the doorway that led into the living room.

"Mama, I came to live with you," I smiled, excited.

"I always knew you were stupid," she said through gritted teeth. "Don't you know if I hadda wanted your ass, I woulda kept you in the first place?"

"Mama, look at me," I said, showing her the bruises on my face and arms. "I really can't take much more of Granny." I tried to think of a reason she might let me stay, a way I could prove to her that I was worth it. "I will help you with the baby, and with the house… and—"

"I don't want you here, you hear me?"

I didn't want to believe her. I hugged her tight, wrapping my arms around her neck. She pushed me off of her as she turned inside. I followed her in, noticing the baby, named Jeremy, lying on the couch. I immediately went over and picked him up. He was a cute baby, half-Caucasian and half-black with dark skin that smelled like baby lotion and soft, curly, black hair. His sweet smile and gentle coos made me forget how jealous I was that Mama wanted him instead of me.

"He's so sweet, Mama."

"Yes, he is," she said, "just like your brother and sister were." I didn't acknowledge how much it hurt me that she insulted me at every chance.

She continued. "If you're gonna stay here, you will have to sleep on the floor in Niki's room. I'm not making anybody give up a bed just because you're here."

"That's fine, Mama, I don't mind. I can just make a pallet. I promise I will fold it all up every morning." I knew that was the best approval I would get from her and I was happy just to be there, to see her and my brother again.

"What did Granny Jack say about you coming here?" Mama asked. "She doesn't know yet. I need you to call and tell her, Mama."

"Hell no, I'm not callin' her," she said. "She's gonna go ape-shit wild when she finds out you're here. She'll probably drive up here and beat your ass again! There's a pay phone down the road. Get to it and call her right now. I don't wanna be gettin' in trouble for kidnappin' or some shit."

The thought of calling Granny Jack and telling her that I was with Mama, the daughter that she despised as much as Mama despised me, almost made me sick to my stomach. Granny had always hated her daughter, and yelled at me whenever I mentioned her. But I told Mama I would be right back. If I didn't do as she said quickly, she might get angry with me and tell me I had to leave for good.

I drove a mile to a dilapidated gas station with a pay phone situated at the end of the gravel lot. I had just enough change to make the call. The phone rang once, then a second time. I secretly hoped that no one would answer and I would just leave a message on the answering machine. But on the third ring, Granny Jack answered.

"Hello?"

"Granny, it's me," I wanted to continue, but my mouth was frozen with fear. "What in the hell are you doin' calling this time of day?" she barked.

There was no way to make it pleasant. I had to say it. "I'm at my mama's. She said I can live with her."

Granny Jack interrupted abruptly. "If you want to live with that piece of trash, then don't come back here! I don't *ever* want to see you here again," she yelled, "but that damn car you're drivin' better be parked in my driveway tonight! It's mine now! I don't ever want to see you again; you're dead to me."

I was so proud to have a car to call my own, a car that I earned through competing in pageants, and now it was being taken away. I was angry; it wasn't fair. I hung up the phone without responding, determined to be brave, to earn Mama's respect and hopefully her love. I drove the mile back to Mama's house, giving myself a pep talk the whole time. *Come on, Angie, don't lose it now. You can do this; you are finally where you belong.*

"Well, we've got to take the car back to Granny's," I said, mimicking Mama's carefree, sarcastic attitude. I didn't want to show her that it bothered me that I had to give the car back; I knew she needed to feel like being with her was more important than having the car.

"Hell no, we're not taking the car back to her. That's your car and I'm gonna use it now."

I felt annoyed and used, but underneath that I was trying to control my sense of panic. If Mama and Granny got into a fight over the car, I knew who would bear the brunt of it – me. Then the kitchen door opened and Dan walked in.

"To what do I owe this sweet surprise?" he said, walking over to greet me with a hug. I leaned into his tall, strong frame, grateful to finally see someone who was happy I was there.

"Tell him what you are doing here," Mama chimed in.

"I came to live with you and Mama." I awaited Dan's response as he looked carefully between the two of us.

"You know I love me some white sugar; I know you'll sweeten things up around here," Dan said jovially.

I felt comforted by his presence because I knew he would treat me with respect, so I explained that I needed help getting the car back to Granny's house. Mama kept ranting about giving the car up, saying that she deserved the car if she was going to have to put up with another kid, but Dan calmed her down.

"You stay home with the baby," he said. "Me and your mama will drive the car back to Granny's."

I was so grateful that I would not have to face Granny Jack. I was afraid that she would hit me and I didn't think I could take another beating that day, or the pain of feeling worthless to her.

That afternoon, while Mama and Dan were returning my car, I waited for the school bus and the return of my siblings. When it came, I ran into the front yard to greet them. I had missed both of my siblings, but Scotty in particular, who was now thirteen, tall and thin, with defined muscles in his arms and legs. It was strange to see him so grown up.

"Sis! When did you get here?" he asked excitedly, hugging me.

"I've been here about two hours, but guess what?" I high-fived him. "I'm not leaving. I get to live with y'all now!" I felt like I was going to float away with excitement.

Niki was eleven now, with long cotton-blonde hair and nearly flawless pale skin. At about five feet and seven inches, she was taller than most kids her age. Despite looking angelic, she was known as one of the meanest kids in the entire Caledonia public school system.

"Fuckin' A! We ain't got room for no more damn people up in this house!" Niki walked into the house without greeting me, slamming the glass storm door behind her.

I was worried. Niki was furious that I was there, probably not wanting to share our mother's already-limited attention, and she hadn't even heard yet that I would be sleeping in her bedroom.

Scotty read the look on my face with ease.

"Don't worry, sis. I'll watch out for you," he promised me. "She's crazy! We've had to go get her from the jailhouse twice already. The first time she stole a car and wrecked it. Cop said he had never seen an eleven-year-old steal a car! The second time we picked her up, she was high as a kite. You shoulda seen her – it was funny as hell!"

Scotty squinted his eyes and mimicked smoking a joint. We both burst into laughter. It felt good to be standing next to my brother and laughing with him. I didn't know why, but despite growing up with Mama, he had always been sweet, caring, and thoughtful. I was so happy that I was there to stay and would never be separated from him again.

Chapter 15

A month later, not one day that had gone by without Mama telling me how she didn't want me there or ridiculing me for being such a goody-goody. I continued to work hard at home and at Caledonia High School so she would love me and respect me, but the only thing I had gained were bad habits.

I started smoking in hopes to gain brownie points with Lisa. I had seen how proud she was of the fact that Niki smoked cigarettes and occasionally marijuana. "My eleven-year-old daughter can smoke like a grown man," she said, letting me know that I didn't meet her standards. It felt like peer pressure, except that pressure was coming from the person who was supposed to be the role model, to tell me how bad smoking was, to lecture me on all of the reasons I should not do it.

Instead Lisa made fun of me when smoking made me feel nauseated. "You're not even inhaling," she sneered. "Can't you do anything right?"

She also mocked me for my lack of a sex life. In contrast to the parents of my friends, who warned their kids about sex and the danger of STDs, Mama seemed obsessed with the fact that, at fifteen and a half, I hadn't had a boyfriend.

In fact, she kept daring me to have sex. But none of the men I'd seen around the house – either Niki's boyfriends or the men Mama slept with behind Dan's back – seemed safe, like the kind of person I'd want to sleep with. I even kept my own cleaning supplies to scrub the bathroom down, fearful of getting herpes through contact with the toilet.

One Friday night, I planned to go out with some friends I met at school, and told Mama that I would be having sex that night. One of the boys, Tam, was cute. We ended up hanging out at a bonfire at someone's house, then went into a bedroom to make-out. Tam was touchy-feely and obviously wanted to have sex. I thought I would be able to do it, but once the moment came, I couldn't go through with it. Irritated, he took me home early. Regardless, the next day I proudly announced to Mama that I had sex with him.

"Oh yeah? Did you bleed?" she asked.

I was confused about why she was asking me this. It didn't occur to me at the time that maybe she had known about Jerry's abuse when I was a kid.

"No, I didn't bleed."

"That's what I thought," she said through a freshly lit cigarette dangling from her lips. "You didn't have sex. You're a little goody-two-shoes chicken shit,"

Niki treated me with the same disrespect and anger that our mama did, complaining about me at every chance. She resented the fact that I was taking up space on her bedroom floor.

"I just want you to know that I hate you being here, bitch," she said every night as I lay down on my pallet.

Because of my new smoking habit, I had developed a cough that annoyed her. I came home from school one day to find everything I'd left in her room – the few articles of clothing I had and a can of Scrubbing Bubbles I kept hidden in the bottom dresser drawer – lying in the hall floor.

"I'm sick of your ass coughing and keeping me up all damn night and I'm sick of not being able to smoke a joint in my own bedroom without you bitching about it!" she yelled. "You don't belong here anyway."

Scotty tried to comfort me. "It's alright, sis. You can sleep in my bedroom."

Even though Scotty's bedroom was smaller and his bed was just a mattress on the floor, moving to his room was like upgrading to a suite. The only thing that bothered me was that there were no curtains or blinds. The next morning, I took thumbtacks and hung towels over the windows. I was pleased with the upgrade, and felt safer besides without Niki's constant threats to hurt me in my sleep.

Despite moving to Scotty's room, my cough got much worse. I was very sick for a couple of weeks and missed a few days of school because I had a fever and a cough that wouldn't stop. Dan had bought me Tylenol and Nyquil, and made me cups of hot tea, but one night around midnight my fever spiked to 103 and Lisa was forced to take me to the ER in Columbus.

"She has pneumonia, get her a breathing treatment, then get her a room," the doctor said, after seeing how hard I was struggling to breathe. "She will have to stay."

"Okay, can I leave now?" Lisa asked.

I was scared; I didn't want to be left alone. So I was grateful when the nurse told her that, since I was a minor, she'd have to stay at least until they found me an inpatient room.

"Damn! You see what you are putting me through?" Lisa yelled. "Why in the hell did you have to pull this bullshit at this time of night?"

"You can go home, Mama. It's okay." I could hardly talk with the oxygen mask strapped to my face. But I didn't want to make her mad enough to cause a scene in the hospital. I was still terrified of orphanages and foster homes, and always tried to avoid anything that may get me put into state custody.

The nurses and doctors treated me well, and Dan came to see me in the hospital every day that week, bringing frozen yogurt, one of my favorite treats. He even brought Scotty once. I waited to see my mama, but she never came.

The morning I was released, Dan picked me up. I had been worried about missing a week of school and had called to have my assignments from the past week delivered to the office. Dan drove me to the school to collect my studies before we went home, then dropped me off and headed to work. Mama was home – and so was Niki, who had been expelled from school for fighting.

"I'm a damn 5th grader, but the girl whose ass I beat is in the damn 10th grade," Niki was boasting as I walked in, punching her left hand with her right fist. "Bam! They oughta expel her ass for being such a damn wuss."

Mama laughed. She hadn't acknowledged the fact that I was home, but I had learned to not act as if it bothered me. I joined them laughing, hoping to start afresh and gain a little more respect from both of them.

"What the fuck are you laughing at?" Niki asked, sitting on the couch smoking a cigarette. "You won't be laughing when I decide to whip your ass!"

I couldn't believe it. I had been home from the hospital less than thirty minutes, I was trying to fit in, and already the harassment was back, coming from someone more than four years younger than me.

"Shut the fuck up," I snapped. "I'm sick of being ridiculed by a total pot head!"

In a flash, Niki leaped from the couch and onto my back as I turned to run from her.

We fought, punching, pulling hair, and biting, up the hallway and back down again.

"You can break each other up," Mama yelled, "but you'd better not break a damn thing in this house."

I thought my best chance was to break free and run out the front door. I had almost made it back into the living room when she grabbed my right leg, picking it up high off the floor and holding it, tightly draped over her arm. I was hopping on my left leg while trying to break her hand loose from where it was intertwined in my hair. We ended up in the front yard, me falling to the ground, pulling Niki down with me. She sat on top of me, punching me in the face.

"See, bitch? I will kill you!" she said as the school bus pulled up.

The school bus pulled up in front of the house and I heard Scotty's voice. I had always been his protector, but now it seemed like the roles were reversed.

"What the fuck are you doing?" he screamed, running towards us. "Get off her, bitch!"

"Get the gun, Scotty!" I yelled. We had several guns in the house, but Scotty's rifle that he kept hidden in his closet was used mostly for shooting birds and squirrels. I knew it would be enough to scare Niki off, though.

Within seconds Scotty emerged from the house and put the end of the barrel against Niki's back.

"Now get off her! You are never gonna hurt her if I'm around!"

She crawled off of me and stood up, pushing the barrel of the gun away from her. Scotty continued to hold the gun and kept it pointed in her direction until she re-entered the house. He helped me up from the ground.

"Come on, sis, let's go somewhere and get you cleaned up." He walked me down the street to a neighbor's house. My nose and lip were bleeding, and I had fresh scratches on my face and arms. But the neighbors, a nice black family down the street, let me lay on their couch and fall asleep while Scotty and the kids played video games.

Niki and I didn't speak to or acknowledge each other for days after that.

Chapter 16

It was Saturday morning in the first week of October and I was glad. Next to Christmas, Halloween was always my favorite holiday. I had happy memories of going trick-or-treating with Renee, dressed up as punk rockers in ripped jeans and teased hair. I always missed her more this time of year, but I still appreciated the refreshing October breeze and the smell of fallen leaves.

Dan had already gone to work, so I decided I would get up and make breakfast in bed for Mama. I fixed Jeremy a bottle and sat him in his carrier in the kitchen with me so he wouldn't wake Mama up. I fried bacon, scrambled eggs, and baked homemade biscuits just like Memaw had taught me. Scotty woke right before breakfast was done cooking and he helped me prepare a beautiful plate that we sat on a TV tray and took to Mama's room. Our plan worked. She woke up and, for the first time since I had been there, she seemed happy to see me.

"You did a really good job on this, Pangie Bear."

It made me happy to hear her call me the old nickname. We all sat in her bed and watched TV together until she finished eating. After breakfast, I gave Jeremy a bath, then spread a blanket on the living room floor and played with him so that Lisa could have a day to herself.

Shortly after noon, right after I finished feeding Jeremy again, Lisa called me to her room where she still sat in bed, filing her fingernails.

"Come sit down here," she said as she patted the mattress right next to her. "I want you to tell me something."

"Okay, Mama." Her voice was softer and sweeter than usual, and I thought something good was going to happen. Maybe she would finally tell me that she was happy I was there.

"What did Jerry Bramble do to you?"

I was stunned by the question and instantly flashed back to the night she lay next to us in the bed while he abused me. "I don't know what are you talking about!"

"Yes, you do!" she snapped. She began to ask cruel, graphic questions regarding the manner in which he did things. "Did he have to tie you up, or did you give it to him willingly?" She added to the other graphics of exactly what he did.

"Mama, you knew about that?" I was stunned.

"Of course I knew," she snapped.

Suddenly I felt like I was in a nightmare, back at the old white house we lived in, trapped again with Jerry. The breeze blowing through the house suddenly felt like the hot air blowing from the box fan sitting on the metal folding chair on that horrible night when I was seven years old.

"Why didn't you do anything to stop him?" I was filled with rage. I had always wondered how she didn't know. Now it turned out she had known the whole time.

"You were right there, Mama," I began to cry. "There was blood on the sheets and on my clothes. You had to have seen it. He threatened to kill me, Mama! How could you let me get hurt like that? Why didn't you stop it?"

She shook her head dismissively. "It was all your fault! Why would I do anything to help such a worthless piece of shit?" There was no remorse in her eyes and her words were cold, piercing me to the core.

I ran across the hallway, sobbing, and locked myself in the room that I shared with my brother. I cried so hard that I hung my head out of the screen-less window and vomited until I was only dry heaving. I fell asleep in the room alone that night. Scotty slept on the couch; I'm not sure if he heard the conversation, but I know he couldn't bear seeing me that way.

The next morning I woke to the sound of Mama's voice. "Come ride with me. I need to go over to a friend's house and pick some clothes up from her."

I was confused by the sudden change in her attitude, but it was not out of character for her to be hateful and then kind. *Perhaps it has just been a horrible nightmare*, I thought. *Maybe I am losing my mind.*

Regardless of what it was, I was just glad it was over. Our family was pretty good at burying things, and I hoped this would be one of those fights that never got discussed again. I got into the car without any more words between us. We drove down the road with the radio blasting, turning onto a gravel road that took us to a small brick house that seemed like it sat in the middle of nowhere.

"You just stay here in the car, I will be right back," she said.

I watched Mama walk to the front door, still silently pleased with myself that she wanted my company on the trip to her friend's house. *Maybe she is trying to make up for what happened the day before,* I thought. But as the door of the house opened, the pleased feeling I had vanished in an instant and turned into sheer terror when Jerry Bramble walked out of the house, looking exactly the same as he had almost a decade earlier.

I felt like I was hallucinating, like I was out of my mind and just could not wake myself from this nightmare again. But it was real. I opened the door and got out of the car. "Mama, please get back in the car," I begged, wanting to vomit.

She began to confront him about the things that he had done to me years earlier. "How many times did you fuck her, Jerry? Do you know that I'm about to send your sorry ass to jail?"

"She's a damn liar," Jerry screamed, pointing at me. "I can't believe you would listen to that piece of shit."

"She's no liar," Mama countered. "I just took her and had a polygraph test done and she passed with flying fucking colors!"

I was stunned at the response from both of them. I didn't even know what a polygraph test was, but I knew I had not been given one.

Jerry began pleading with Lisa. "Please don't press charges. You would ruin me. Besides, it's been too long; there's no way you can prove a thing!"

Lisa began laughing, the laugh I recognized from right before she did something awful like slicing someone's tires or pouring sugar into their gas tank. She strutted back to the car with a proud strut.

"Now get your ass in the car!" she said to me. I didn't move. "Mama, why did you do that?"

"You need to calm down and stop that damn heavin' and squallin'. I got that bastard scared now," she said, continuing to laugh.

For the first time, I finally believed that she had meant every bad thing she had ever said to me. All the times she said she hated me… that she did not want me, had never wanted me… that I was worthless… it was all true. It was even worse than finding out that she had stood by and let me be abused by this horrible creature for three years of my childhood. And I also knew that I had to stop living in a fantasy world, stop expecting my mother to love me, and start thinking about what my next move would be. I couldn't rely on her. Where would I turn instead?

"What the hell are you standin' there like a stupid idiot for? Use your damn head and get in the car," she said, revving the engine.

It was a long ride home.

The Body: 3

As a hospice nurse, I had encountered too many deaths to count. On many occasions I had witnessed agonizing, angry, or sometimes downright mean looks disappear from the faces of those who took their last breath, to be immediately replaced with a look of peace and contentment. I had hoped I might see such a look on Lisa's face. In life, I had often seen her smile, her eyes twinkling when she played with Scotty and Niki or flirted one of her boyfriends. I had longed for that look from her, but her eyes always turned cold and expressionless when she looked at me. She used to make me sit at the table where everyone else was eating, but not allow me to eat.

"If you keep begging, you won't get to eat tomorrow, either," she'd say, staring at me until I sat in silent hunger. When dinner was over, she made me feed the leftovers to the dogs, taunting me by saying she'd rather the dogs have the food than give it to me.

Once, when she had made my favorite oatmeal chocolate-chip cookies, she left them on the table with orders not to eat any. After everyone went to bed, I crept out of my bedroom to the kitchen to steal a cookie. Lisa walked into my bedroom a few minutes later to find me eating the cookie in bed. I tried to hide it under my sheets, but she found it and grabbed me, shaking me and smacking me on the head, all the while looking at me with that proud, cold face.

In the past, just one look from her could make me anxious. I was always throwing up as a child. A symptom, as I later learned, of PTSD. Even as an adult, flashbacks and memories had the power to make me nauseous. My daughters had a similar problem. When they were confronted with unpleasant memories, they felt sick to their stomachs. Sometimes they couldn't sleep without the light on, something else I'd suffered from when I was young. Even though I'd tried, as a mother, to shield them from all the abuse I'd suffered, they had undergone their own versions of trauma. Was PTSD something I had passed down to them?

Now, when I looked up from examining Lisa's hand, I saw that her right eye was partially open. For a moment, it seemed as though she was staring directly at me with the same expression she always wore when she looked at me, the same look she gave me when she revealed she'd known all along about Jerry's abuse. But now, instead of feeling like vomiting, I felt only sadness and anger. Sadness that her body had lain in a house, alone and rotting for at least two entire days before she was found. Anger that, now that she was dead, I'd never get the chance to see her look on me kindly.

Chapter 17

After she forced me to see Jerry again, I knew I wasn't safe with Mama, no matter how much I wanted to be near my brother and sister. I could barely stand to look her in the face, realizing that she had known all along about the abuse I'd suffered at Jerry's hands. And it seemed like the feeling was mutual. She began giving me even more evil looks, telling me that I ruined her life and that she wished I was dead. I felt hopeless and worthless around her, and I began to make a plan to get away.

But I also knew I wasn't welcome back at Granny Jack's, not after how I'd left things with her. Memaw had moved into a small mobile home on Granny and Paw's property, so living with her was practically the same thing as living with Granny. Pete was gone and I didn't know how to get in touch with the Harrisons.

I'd begun working, however, pageant coaching a little girl named Holly. I taught her how to model and helped her with her hair and makeup before shows. Her mother, Cheryl, wasn't particularly warm with me but her grandmother, Jean, seemed to like me. Was there a chance they'd take me in if I got desperate? I had never told anyone what my situation was like at home. But Jean had started catching on that things weren't so good after seeing me bruised a few times. She began questioning how I was treated at Granny Jack's house and at Mama's.

I realized what I really wanted was family. Even though I hadn't seen him since I was ten, I missed my dad, Eddie Leech, and his sister, my aunt Tammy. *Surely,* I thought, *if I get in touch them, between the two of them, I would be able to find a place to live and people to love.*

I spent all day working up the nerve to approach Mama, finally coming into her room in the early afternoon while she was watching TV on the bed.

"Mama, do you know where my dad is?"

She looked at me without emotion. "Who are you talking about?"

I thought I had asked a straightforward question, so her response left me confused and irritated. "Eddie Leech! You know, my daddy?"

"He's not your daddy, you fool," she said, not looking up from the television set. "What?" I had told myself all day to remain calm in this conversation, no matter what, but now I felt dizzy, like I was going to vomit again.

"Yeah, your real daddy's name was Daniel Miller, and he's dead."

I didn't believe her. Mama lied to me – and to everyone else – all the time. Once I heard her on the phone, telling a bill collector that she couldn't pay right away because her father had been in a traumatic car accident. She made up vivid details off the cuff, including fabricating the image of a three-year-old child lying dead on the hood of the car. To get out of obligations to me, she had made up fake lung cancer and brain tumors and told me she only had six months to live. I was sure that she was doing the same thing now, trying to make me believe I was optionless.

"He was killed when you were three months old," Mama continued. "Murdered on the Tombigbee River. One of his buddies knocked him unconscious and he fell out of the boat. Undercurrent got him."

"Stop fucking lying to me!" I yelled. "I just want to know where Eddie Leech is! I know you hate me. I thought you'd be glad I want to find my dad!"

"It's no lie," she said, finally looking me in the eye. "Eddie was a trucker. He left on a truck trip right after we got married and didn't come back for months. And I loved Daniel; he was my true love. By the time Eddie got back home, I was already pregnant with your ass."

The past two days – Mama forcing me to talk about Jerry's abuse, dragging me to see him again, and then telling me that the man I had always thought was my father was actually not – felt like I'd been watching a movie, and the ending was a sick twist. Was this why Eddie had disappeared from my life? Why I'd never seen Aunt Tammy again? I had so many questions, but the lump in my throat was so sharp I felt like it would rip my throat open if I tried to speak.

"Where is Daniel's family?" I finally blurted out. "I'm going to find them! Someone there will tell me the truth."

I still wasn't sure if I could believe her. But if this man Daniel really was my dad, maybe his family would take me in. Maybe they were wonderful people who had spent years looking for me. I immediately envisioned a tall, blonde woman and her handsome husband with silver-sprinkled

109

hair greeting me, wrapping me up in their arms, maybe even crying and telling me how long they had searched for me.

But Mama dashed my hopes when she spoke again.

"Don't waste your time looking for them! I tried to give you to them when you were five years old and they didn't want you either." She gave a short, sharp laugh. "His family are all Mennonites. Real weird people who think they are the only ones goin' to heaven. All the women have to wear long dresses and little black caps on their head with their bangs slicked back in a butt-cut."

"In fact," she continued, "They think their son died *because* he had you."

"Because he had me?" I was shocked and confused.

"Yeah, out of wedlock," she said. "It's a sin, you know, to have kids without being married. They called you Sin Child."

Part of me knew she could be lying to me. But another part heard her words, took them in, and they became an answer to the question I'd always had. Why could no one love me? And why, when I found love with Renee, with Pete, with the Harrisons, was it taken away from me?

Maybe Mama was right. Maybe I was worthless. Maybe God had created me as a sin child.

Chapter 18

The next Sunday, while Dan cooked spaghetti for dinner and Mama napped on the couch with Jeremy, I was so happy to see Memaw pull into the driveway. I hadn't seen her in nearly three months and ran to her car, feeling like I was running toward my angel of mercy as she opened the door and stepped out. I immediately embraced her, instantly comforted by the familiar smell of Estee Lauder perfumed powder that she used every day.

"I missed you so much, Memaw!"

"I missed you too, baby," she said, walking me toward the front door of the house.

"Memaw, come on in here and see the baby." Mama greeted her with the sweet voice that she only used when she wanted something. "He has grown so much."

Memaw walked into the wood-paneled living room and took Jeremy, now eight months old, from Mama's arms.

"I'm sorry I didn't get to come see you while you were in the hospital, angel," Granny said, cuddling Jeremy on the couch while looking at me with sadness. "You sure look like you lost a lot of weight."

"It's okay, Granny. I'm much better—" I began to say.

"—I had to wait up all night long with her in the emergency room until they got her admitted!" Mama interrupted, her sugary tone reverting to her usual bitterness. "I was tired as hell and had to go to work the next afternoon. She's done nothin' but cause me trouble ever since she's been here!"

"Now Lisa, what on earth has that child done to you?" Memaw asked, peering at where Mama sat near her on the loveseat.

"I hate that damn little wench!" Mama said. "I have enough to do around here without taking care of her!"

Since I'd come back from Granny Jack's, I hadn't said a mean word to Mama. But now, as she humiliated me in front of my favorite grandmother, I wanted to hurt her.

"You think you are so good," I stood, trembling, staring at her from eyes that wouldn't blink. "You are not! You are an evil, two-faced liar… and I hate you for that!" Tears rolled freely down my cheeks as I thought of all the times I had lied for her – to Dan, to my siblings, to other folks – covering up her lies and infidelity. "Tell Dan. Tell him what you do when he is at work. Tell him about all your boyfriends!"

I knew Dan was in the kitchen, just a few feet away, and hoped that would hear my words, that he'd leave Mama feeling rejected and broken, just like she'd made me feel.

"Like who?" Mama asked, pretending to chuckle but not moving her eyes from my face.

"We can start with Jeff, and how you got that car parked in the driveway!" Jeff was one of Mama's friends who visited her whenever Dan wasn't home. I had heard her

112

having phone sex with him once and only recently he had given Mama a brown Lincoln Continental.

"Or how about Mike?" Mike was almost seven feet tall and weighed over 500 pounds. He had salt-and-pepper hair with sideburns and a slicked-back pompadour like Elvis.

As soon as Mama charged toward me, I knew this had been the wrong thing to say. But it was too late. She grabbed my collar and gripped it tightly around my neck.

"You ungrateful little bitch! I'm so sick of you!"

I heard a door slam and saw Dan coming towards us. He had heard everything. He had always been kind to me and I'd never seen him be violent with Mama, but my body froze, expecting an attack.

Memaw tried to get between us, grabbing Mama's hands in an attempt to loosen them from my shirt, but Mama pushed her to the side. She slapped me across my face, first one side then the other, then grabbed the back of my shirt, ripping it from the neck halfway down my back.

I finally fought my way out of her grasp and ran into the kitchen. Mama followed me, backing me up against a cabinet and standing between me and the door leading to the carport. I had nowhere else to go and, as I turned to face her, she picked up the pot of boiling water that Dan had going for the spaghetti noodles.

"Lisa! *Put that down*!" Dan said as he re-entered the kitchen with Memaw right behind him.

Mama looked between Dan and me as if she couldn't decide who to dump the pot of water onto. He approached her slowly, took the pot of water out of her hands, and dumped it in the sink, then left the room.

I slumped down the wall, crying and shaking on the kitchen floor.

Memaw ran over to me, wrapped her arms around me, and whispered, "I can't take this, I'm sorry baby. I have to go. I love you."

In just seconds I heard her car backing out of the driveway and heading away from the house. Dan, who always walked away from an argument before it could get too heated, had gone back to the bedroom. I was alone with Mama.

"See what you did? See?" Mama repeated, grabbing me by my cheeks and pulling me up from the kitchen floor. She kicked the backs of my legs and tugged at my hair, forcing me out into the carport.

"Get in the fucking car! I'm gonna kill you, you no-good piece of shit!"

"I'm sorry, Mama," I begged as she shoved me in the car. I didn't know where she was going to take me, but I thought she might just make good on her threat this time. "Please forgive me. Where are we going?"

"I'm sending you away," Lisa said, still in a screaming rage, a plethora of curse words streaming from her mouth. We drove to the old abandoned gas station down the road. It had a working payphone and I often walked there to call Memaw or to schedule appointments for modeling classes that I taught.

When we got there, Lisa barreled out the door, toward the phone.

"Is this the Columbus Police Department? I have an emergency," she said after dialing. "I have a no-good fifteen-year-old daughter."

I stood beside her, blood coming from my mouth and nose, staining the ripped collar of my shirt. My face felt swollen and my eyes burned.

On the other end of the phone, a man asked questions. "Ma'am, what has she done?"

"She's just useless!"

"Is she a threat to you or anyone around you?"

"No, but I just beat the hell out of her and I'm about to do it again if somebody don't come get her!"

"Please, Mama," I dropped to my knees, not even noticing the rough gravel scratching my legs. "You can't send me away." If Mama was calling the authorities to come get me, where would they take me? I remembered what Granny Jack and Paw had said about orphanages and foster homes. Were those my only options now?

"Is she on drugs?" the police officer asked.

"Hell no," Mama said, annoyed, "she's just a little goody-two-shoes chicken shit."

"Ma'am, has she ever been in trouble with law or had any trouble at school?"

"Not that I know of, but you people need to come get her. I don't want her at my house. I don't want her at all!"

I didn't hear the officer's response but Lisa cursed the police as she slammed the phone back on the receiver.

"Goddamn no-good cops! See, the police don't even want you, and you know what kind of scum bags they take in!"

From my place, sitting in the gravel, I didn't respond to her, or even cry. I was numb. I felt as though I had left my own body and was watching all of this from afar. Lisa began pacing back and forth in front of the pay phone.

"Who have you been teaching modeling to? Give me their numbers," she demanded.

I did not want her to call my students' parents, I didn't want them to know that I was so worthless I'd been turned down by the police. But she snatched my hair until I gave up the number for Cheryl, Holly's mom. While she dialed the number, I watched, praying that they would not answer. I just wanted to be left alone. I wanted to start walking down the road and wander so far into the woods that no one would ever find me. No one, I thought, would care anyway.

After a couple of rings, someone answered on the other end. It was Jean, Holly's grandmother.

"I just wanted y'all to know that I just beat the hell out of this no-good kid you think is so great! Don't worry about calling the police," she said angrily, "they don't even want her!" Mama continued to tell Jean how no one had ever wanted me and how they just needed to come and get me.

Finally Mama turned to me. "Come to the phone, you little bitch! They wanna talk to you," she hissed through clenched teeth, shoving the phone in my hand then stalking away.

I stood up slowly and put the phone to my ear. I didn't know what to say, though, didn't know how to defend myself from Mama's accusations. "I'm here," I muttered.

"Are you okay, honey?" Jean asked with a shaky voice. "Is she telling the truth?"

"I'm sorry, I don't know why she called you. I will be okay," I said, trying to hide the shakiness in my voice. I worried that they would fire me after Mama's performance on the phone, that my reputation in the pageant circles would be ruined. Not only did I need the money I got from coaching Holly, but I didn't want to be associated with my mother or my grandmother – both legendary for their tempers.

"This is not the first time she has called, honey," Jean said slowly. "We have discussed it here several times anyway. Why don't you just come and live with us? I can't stand the thought of you being hurt like that."

She wasn't surprised by Mama's call; she already knew how bad things were for me. I was so embarrassed someone had seen my vulnerability. But what choice did I have?

"Okay," I agreed. "When can you get me?"

"We don't need any confrontation with your mama," she said. "Get on the bus just like you are going to school tomorrow morning. She is not going to let you have your belongings, so just put whatever you can in a bag. One of us will pick you up at the gas station right down the road from the schoolhouse. Be there at 9:00 in the morning. One of us will be waiting for you in a red car."

When I got off the phone, I felt relieved. But I was still afraid of what Mama would do. Even though Mama had made it clear she did not want me, I felt like she also really didn't want anyone taking me – especially people who might actually care.

Chapter 19

The next morning, I packed all of my belongings into a single black trash bag and left the house while everyone still slept. I walked down the road, praying to the sky that Jean had sent someone. A long, crooked limb lay in the gully alongside the road and I stopped and picked it up. I swung the stick in front of me for the two-mile journey, trying to lighten my own mood by pretending I was a true hobo, everything I owned in little red bandanna tied on the end of the stick instead of my trash bag. But instead of feeling carefree, my face and arms were bruised and scratched, my ribs ached, and my heart was numb.

If nobody showed up, I had decided I would hitchhike into Columbus and figure something out from there. I had packed a small blanket and small worn out pillow just in case I had to sleep in one of the abandoned warehouses around. But Jean was true to her word; the red car she mentioned was parked in front of the convenience store.

I had met Jean a few years before at a pageant. She was hard to miss – a bleach-blonde woman with never a hair out of place, heavy eye makeup, and lavish jewelry on top of expensive clothing. A frequent judge, Jean had even judged me in a pageant or two before formally introducing herself and asking if I would coach her granddaughter Holly.

I was relieved as we pulled into the driveway of the Tupelo house where I taught Holly modeling. The three-bedroom home was in a nice neighborhood and was always clean, with a well-manicured yard – things I associated with safety and comfort. Jean's daughter and son-in-law, Cheryl and Wayne, greeted me and helped me find a place to stash my stuff.

There was no extra bedroom, so we created a makeshift bedroom in the attic room above the garage. A room with a low slanted ceiling and no windows, it was filled with Holly's toys, stuffed animals, and a small television that sat on a toy box. There was just enough room to place a day bed on one side. Sleeping in there made me feel claustrophobic and I nearly rammed my head through the sheet-rock ceiling more than once, but it was better by far than sleeping in an abandoned building.

That night, Granny began calling their house, threatening to "blow my head off." Granny ranted that I was just horrible and ungrateful for everything she had done for me and how much money she had spent on pageants. She said she'd rather see me dead than embarrassing the family by living somewhere else, although that was nothing new. I think she was worried I would tell the whole truth about how I was treated at home, and she would look bad or even get in trouble for drawing a check off me for so many years.

The threatening phone calls went on for a couple days and I was afraid that Wayne, Cheryl, and Jean would not be able to take it. But, although they were concerned about their family's safety, they were very nice to me. Jean even told me to call her "Mama Jean." And the threatening calls just died after a couple of days.

House rules were established very soon. In return for free rent, I was to do all of my own laundry and wash the household linens such as sheets, bath towels, and wash cloths. I would also babysit Holly when needed, while still coaching her for modeling, helping design her pageant clothes, and doing her hair and makeup at pageants.

This didn't seem like such a bad deal at first. Holly, a beautiful child with long auburn hair, was a gifted student in Montessori School. But she was also very spoiled. Cheryl and Jean continuously praised her for being smart and beautiful and allowed her to interrupt anyone at any given moment. She got a 'Holly bag' every single day, a daily gift bag which could range from a bag of candies and treats to clothes or shoes. I was so happy to have a place to stay that I didn't feel jealous of how differently she was treated.

But I also found that, outside of this work, I would need to get a job so I could pay for meals at schools, personal items, clothes, etc. I began working part-time at the Buzy Bee, a convenience store in a town about ten miles south of Tupelo, owned by Mama Jean's ex-husband, Tommy. Mama Jean taught me to run the cash register and gas pumps, to stock the shelves and do the ordering.

The Buzy Bee was known as a place where anyone could get anything. While we ordered cigarettes from regular vendors, we also bought cases of stolen cigarettes that came in through the back door. A black van would pull to the back of the store, always after the sun had set. Every cigarette carton was stamped with a serial number on the end of the box. As soon as we received the special cases of cigarettes, we peeled off the end of the carton that was stamped and burned it before we could stock them on the rack that hung directly above the cash register. When we rang up the stolen cigarettes, we had to ring them up as food items, so that nothing strange appeared in our records.

We also sold beer to minors and on Sundays, which was just as illegal in the Bible Belt of Mississippi as selling drugs. The fact that I was a minor selling beer was even worse. Tommy and Mama Jean trained me to look for certain behaviors that might indicate undercover agents. If someone was dressed too nicely, or kept looking out the front windows, or if there were any strange cars in the parking lot, I wasn't supposed to sell beer to them.

At the time, I did not understand the seriousness of the situation. I thought the worst thing that could happen would be for the store to get fined and maybe the owner of the store would be arrested. Years later, when I shared this story with a friend, she told me I could have been prosecuted and gone to jail for these crimes… that Tommy and Mama Jean had put me in a lot of danger. But at the time, all I knew was they were adults, I trusted them, and even if I hadn't, I relied on them for everything.

Chapter 20

Mama Jean and I had decided to wait until the following week to get me registered for school. We knew we had to devise a story so that the school did not notify the Department of Human Services that I was not living with my legal guardians and thought it would only add suspicion if I showed up for my first day at a new school scratched and bruised. That Monday, we drove to the biggest school I'd ever seen: Tupelo High School.

Based on the first letter of my last name, I was assigned an advisor, Camille Caples, a petite lady with short salt-and-pepper hair. She greeted us with a warm smile when we entered her office and listened pleasantly as we delivered our well-planned story to get me enrolled in school. Mama Jean pretended to be my grandmother, which made Mrs. Caples ask us why she was registering me for school and not my parents.

"Where are your parents? Do you have brothers and sister who will be other Tupelo schools?"

I decided to go with statements that weren't technically lies, but also weren't the truth Mrs. Caples was asking for.

"My mom works out of town, ma'am, and my father is deceased."

When the meeting was over, Mama Jean left and I went to my first class at yet another new school.

I was assigned to Frances Ellis' classroom for study hall. Like Mrs. Caples, she had a lot of questions for me the first day, but it didn't take long for me to form a bond with her. Since it was the middle of the semester, there weren't any seats left; I sat on the floor directly behind her desk and spent the twenty-minute class period talking to Mrs. Ellis. She always had questions for me about my family and my current living situation. "Who are your friends?" she asked. "What do you do in your spare time?"

"I don't have time for friends. I have to work. I'm okay though," I assured her, trying to fake a cheerful attitude.

I slowly met people and made friends, although they might not have been the healthiest for me at the time. They were different than my friends at Calhoun Academy. Back at the academy, my friends were all very conservative, rooted in Christian morals and beliefs. They would never have thought about drinking or smoking pot. But here in Tupelo, most of my friends lived slightly scandalous lifestyles.

Most of them were much better-off than I was, as well, although that wouldn't have been difficult. Megan, Perry, Tasha, and Amanda all had what seemed to be endless cash flow from their parents, but they all treated me well. They invited me to their houses for bonfires, over to swim in their pools, or even to cruise in their boats on Pickwick Lake.

Perry was the most levelheaded one. She didn't smoke or drink… much. She was funny, the kind of person who could crack a room up with just one comment. The group of us liked to ride around the loop in Tupelo, by Taco Bell, and the warehouse district, listening to the blaring radio in her Chrysler LeBaron.

Amanda, whose dad was an attorney, seemed to enjoy minor shoplifting for sport. It was a thrill for her. We ate at Cracker Barrel restaurant once with Megan's parents. After the meal, Amanda came out with her pursed stuffed. She handed out a snow-globe to Megan's mom and a framed inspirational saying to Megan's dad. Then she gave friendship rings that she pulled from the inside of her cheek to Megan and me.

Tasha's parents, who had family money and owned various businesses around Tupelo, didn't know that their daughter dated black guys. One night, she invited me to go with her to pick up some friends. When we got to the house, I was surprised to see that her friends were two men in their thirties, both with gold teeth and beards. As soon as we pulled out, we all started smoking pot in the car, riding down Hwy 6 toward Pontotoc. Just as we reached the outskirts of Tupelo, the blue lights started to flash behind us. I began to freak out.

"Oh my god, what should we do? We're gonna get arrested!"

"Shut up," one of the guys said. "Just keep quiet, and… here." He handed me a couple of clear sandwich bags, some full of white powder, others full of weed. "Put these down your pants."

The police officer came up to the side of the car. Tasha rolled the window down, releasing what must have been a cloud of pot-scented air. I kept my eyes straight ahead, too afraid to look at him.

"You know why I pulled you over?" he asked.

"Because I swerved?" Tasha said uncertainly.

"Yes, ma'am. Why did you swerve?"

"I dropped a CD," she began to explain. "I reached down to get it and when I looked up, I had crossed the line, so I jerked back."

The officer asked for her license, then looked in the back of the car to see the guys. Then, with just a warning to be careful, he let her go.

He must have recognized her name, I realized later, and let her go because of her father's reputation. It took me years to put this together, though, because I had never been anyone whose name was valued. It also took me years to realize that, if we had been arrested, as I was the one holding all the drugs, I would have taken all the blame.

One night, while Scotty was visiting, Tasha took the two of us out to a house in the country outside Tupelo. I didn't know anyone, but with Scotty there, I felt safe. Everyone was smoking pot and a stranger passed me a joint.

"Here, take a hit of this," he said. I took it, assuming it was pot like I'd smoked before. I took a big puff and held it in for a few seconds. Then the world around me began to slide forward, like I was running backwards. I slammed into the wall behind me and slid down to land on the floor. I sat there for what felt like forever.

"Sis! Sis!" Scotty said, touching my face.

"C'mon man, straighten up," Tasha laughed, "quit acting like this."

The next thing I remember, I woke up at Tasha's house. Scotty was gone. I didn't remember how I got there.

"What happened?" I asked.

"That was cocaine, you fool," Tasha said. "You weren't supposed to hold it in like that."

Megan's mom was a nurse at the local health department and she made sure all of us girls were on birth control whether we needed it or not. Megan had a near unlimited supply of cash and a brand-new Chevy Camaro. She never wanted for anything but was very generous with her money, even paying for my food most of the time when we went out. Her parents treated me the same way, never making me feel like I was a burden and never asking awkward questions that I didn't know how to answer. But I didn't want to take any chances. Most of the time when I stayed at Megan's, I snuck in after her parents were in bed and sometimes I would sleep in the floor between the bed and the wall so that I couldn't be seen.

Those girls were fearless. They had each other's backs. And if I'd let them in, they probably would have had mine, too. I'm sure they suspected things about my home life, especially with how often I ended up staying at their houses. But I never talked to them about my family. I just wanted to be normal, to fit in, and be appreciated for who I was, not pitied for what I didn't have.

Chapter 21

The only bathroom in the Buzy Bee was in a padlocked back room that Tommy used sometimes for meetings he wanted to keep secret. I didn't know for certain, but I thought perhaps he was making drug deals in the space. I only went back there when I needed to use the restroom, a single-stall attached to a large, empty room with a concrete floor. But generally I was so scared of this dungeon that sometimes I held my bladder until I thought it would burst.

"Now I'm gonna be in the back with some friends," Tommy said. "You just stay here and take care of the store. Make sure you don't open that padlock while we are back here. You're such a good girl, I know I can trust you to do that, right?"

Even though I felt he was doing something illegal, I was proud that he trusted me. Tommy, a thin man with black hair and a charming personality that all of his numerous girlfriends seemed to love, did not trust people easily. I had heard stories of what happened to people who got in his way or tried to rat him out, and I knew that when they were still married, he had broken Mama Jean's foot by pushing her down a flight of stairs. I had even seen him myself pick fights with customers when he was drunk. But this background of violence made it more noticeable that he was never aggressive or rude with me. He always told me I could get whatever I wanted to eat or drink from the store without having to pay for it. He gave me free cigarettes, too, and sometimes an extra $20.

Despite my gratitude towards Tommy and Mama Jean, I didn't really enjoy my job at the Buzy Bee. I usually got there right after school every weekday, working until the store closed at 10 pm or midnight, and then worked another afternoon/evening shift on Saturdays. Most of my job involved running the cash register, ordering and stocking goods for the store, controlling the gas pumps, and cleaning. Sometimes Megan or the other girls came by to buy beer, which I sold them illegally, charging them a little extra so I could keep more money for myself. We also bought food stamps for $.50 on the dollar and sold pickled eggs and pickled pig feet from behind the counter. They were kept in glass gallon jars with a white screw on lid. Every time I removed the top to dip one out, I wanted to throw up.

The store atmosphere wasn't helped by the fact that I was surrounded by the shrill beeping of the gas pumps, the yelling matches between local drug dealers and drunks, the fights I had to break up to keep our shelves from being overturned. I constantly forced people away from the padlocked door in the back.

"Read the damn sign! NO PUBLIC RESTROOMS! Now leave that damn padlock alone or I'm gonna call the cops," I snapped.

The trickiest part was overseeing the gambling. Even though it was illegal in Mississippi, we had four poker machines that sat in the back-right corner of the store behind a wooden lattice piece like a cage. Some of our regulars would sit there for hours, only getting up to go outside and sniff cocaine or smoke a joint. Every now and then someone would pull out a homemade tin foil package and sniff the white powdery substance or light a joint right there in the store, acting no different than if they were smoking a cigarette.

At closing time, it was difficult to make the gamblers get off the poker machines, especially if they were stoned or drunk. Mama Jean had given me a taser gun and told me to carry it with me. Everyone else who worked there had a real gun, but I felt invincible with my taser. I looped the attached strap around my wrist and walked to the back, twirling it with the attitude and presence, the way the Rifleman carried his rounded lever-action Winchester.

"Time to get off now. Follow me to the front and I will get you paid," I said to our customers, counting out cash from the register. I was too naive to realize how easily I could have been robbed of all the cash in those three torn-green pleather-bank bags.

On Friday and Saturday nights we closed down at midnight. After getting the store ready for the next day, I left the store, usually with no less than $15,000 in cash. The sheriff of Shannon, a kind man who reminded me of Santa Claus, came to meet me when it was about time for me to leave, making sure I got the money safely into the car and then following me until I crossed over the county line. I was always impressed with the fact that he came to help me, even when he wasn't on duty. Three years later, this nice sheriff was shot from behind, execution style, just before sunrise. I have always found it unusual that, out of the sixty-four slain officers that year, his still remains the only case unsolved.

By Christmas of 1993, I heard Mama Jean, Cheryl, and Wayne discussing Tommy's legal situation daily. The story was that Tommy had been involved in drug rings, stolen cigarettes, and missing people. When I went into work one afternoon after school, Mama Jean and Tommy told me they needed to talk to me.

"There are some rumors going around about me, Angie," he said. "Lots of stuff bein' said. Even though it's not all true, it looks like I'm gonna have to do a little time. I have some real good friends that kept me out of the big pen, but it looks like I'm gonna have to do a little time in the county jail."

The only person I'd ever known who'd been in prison was my biological grandfather, Granny Jack's ex-husband Larry Alred, the guy who'd been on Mississippi's most wanted list. When I lived with Mama, we visited him from time to time and he told me stories about how he used to con mostly elderly folks out of money. I remembered how much I hated listening to his stories, and how disgusted I was by him. But I didn't feel that way about Tommy. Even though I believed he was guilty, I hated the thought of this nice man who'd taken care of me going to jail.

"I'm gonna need you to help your Mama Jean take care of this store for me," he said. "You know I trust you two more than anybody else, even my own kids. You can do that for me, right?"

Tommy always made me feel so important, so I worked hard to make sure everything was taken care of. Only a few days later, I received the news he had been arrested and taken to jail on relatively minor charges of buying and selling stolen cigarettes.

Chapter 22

Between working at the Buzy Bee, coaching Holly, and going to school, I wasn't sleeping much. When I did sleep, I had nightmares. Sometimes about Jerry and Boey, sometimes just Jerry, and sometimes it was Mama or Granny beating me. It got so bad that, at one point, I became suicidal.

I checked into a motel and took an entire bottle of Tylenol PM, thinking that I would fall into a deep slumber and never wake up. After swallowing thirty pills, I lay in the musty smelling bed waiting for sleep to overtake me. Instead, my head swam and I began to hallucinate. I felt disoriented and became violently sick at my stomach. The night seemed to last forever and I never fell asleep. I phoned the front desk when morning came and asked to extend my stay for another day. I felt like I was on a horrible drunk that wouldn't end. After the second night, I didn't have enough money to stay for a third, so I went back to Mama Jean's and told them I had the flu. For an entire week I only woke long enough to vomit and stayed so dizzy I would sleep in the bathroom floor between the toilet and the tub. I never told them what had really happened.

Even when I didn't want to kill myself, the flashbacks of abuse were a daily struggle. Anytime I could get my hands on a bottle of vodka, I would drink my woes away. I would often walk down to the depot grocery store and look for anyone who I thought would go into the liquor store across the street and buy me a bottle if I gave them a few extra bucks. I soon started taking over-the-counter energy supplements that we sold at the Buzy Bee. The pills made me shaky, affecting my handwriting, but they kept me awake for class. One day I took an entire pack. Afterwards, I kept touching my head. It was tingling all over, like a spider-web was growing out of my scalp. Mrs. Ellis confronted me, sending me to the office. I explained to her that I was taking these pills to help keep me awake and told her a little bit about why I had trouble sleeping at night, explaining about Boey the snake but not about Jerry's other abuse.

The very next day, Mrs. Ellis told me that she had a friend who was a psychologist and she thought he may could help. She explained to me that she was worried because she felt like I had to deal with too many bad things.

"Sweetie, I don't know how you have made it this far with no help," she admitted. "I can't stand the thought of you not being able to sleep at night and I don't know how to help you."

I was hesitant, but she promised to go with me, to sit by me the entire time. I didn't want to hurt her feelings, so I went.

That was how I met Joe Ed Morris, a psychologist in Tupelo. He had bushy brown hair and sported a huge mustache that curled at the corners of his mouth. At first, he didn't seem like he had much personality, handing me a small booklet with questions in it.

"Answer all these questions and then we will talk."

I was beginning to wonder what I had gotten myself into.

When I began reading the booklet, I thought the questions were ridiculous. One of the questions was "do you like to watch candles burn?" which I could answer on a scale of 1–5. This made me a little paranoid because I liked to watch any kind of fire: candles, cigarette lighters, bonfires… I had even, in an odd way, enjoyed watching the fire at the duplex when Niki burned it down years earlier. But my mother had actually burned down several houses and I was afraid Joe Ed would label me as crazy.

Mrs. Ellis could tell from the look on my face that I was ready to run out the door. She encouraged me to stay.

"He is going to help you," she said. "You have to trust me."

When it came time to go into his office with him, she came with me and sat next to me the entire time.

I didn't trust him, but I didn't trust many men. I did, however, begin to talk about my past, opening up about the sexual abuse, the beatings, and – worst of all – my mother's hatred and neglect. At the time, though, I didn't use the word 'abuse.' I only talked about the details of specific events, explaining my nightmares and my fears.

Joe Ed told me he wanted to play a tape for me. As it played, he explained that he wanted me to listen to it every night when I went to bed, repeating the words to myself. He asked me to promise to do this for a week. After a nudge from Mrs. Ellis, I agreed.

Soon what I had thought was a complete hoax, some sort of witchery, actually began to help me. Somehow I always felt better after talking about my problems. I slept better too. After Joe Ed gave me the recorded tape to listen to, Mrs. Ellis took me to Walmart and bought me a cassette player of my own.

Each night, I lay on the half daybed that sat against the low wall of the attic and listened to the tape as Joe Ed instructed.

There is cool air blowing on my head.

There is warm blood running through my veins. I am safe. I am not afraid.

I repeated these words again and again until I was asleep.

Chapter 23

Every Saturday Mama Jean and I made a trip to the jail to visit Tommy. We took all of the receipts from the store along with invoices from vendors, and for 30 minutes, Tommy signed checks and I prepared them to be delivered. He also inquired about who had been in and if there were any new people asking for him.

I didn't like seeing him in jail. I had known him to be so free, always working deals and trying to make moves on attractive women. Seeing him confined made me sad. Even though I knew Tommy had a dangerous side, it had always been hidden from me. With his joking kindness to me, his physical presence, and the fact that he always had a gun on him, he had a way of making me feel safe even when I was probably in danger. I wanted to please him, to be worthy of the trust he'd placed in me.

Within the first few weeks of Tommy being in jail, Mama Jean began to see someone else. She and Tommy had been divorced for years but they continued to have an affair and he supported her financially. But now that he was out of the picture, she had long talks on the phone late into the night with Tommy's best friend, Mike.

One of Tommy's underlings, Mike, was best known around the store for doing time in prison for selling narcotics without prescriptions and exchanging prescription drugs for 'favors' from the storefront of the pharmacy he owned. He had thick, silver hair that illuminated his red face, flushed from his constant drinking. He always wore a suit and tie and he drove brand new Cadillacs and Buicks. Cold shivers ran down my spine when he smiled, a grin that looked mocking and malicious to me. But Mama Jean laughed like a giggly schoolgirl every time she was around him. Their constant flirting and touching was enough to make me gag.

Each day at 5 pm, Tommy called us at the store for five minutes. Mama Jean talked to him on the phone, catching him up on the day's events. Near the end of each call, Mama Jean placed her big leather purse over her shoulder and put her sunglasses on so that she would not waste a single minute getting out of there.

"I love you too, Tommy," she said. "Be careful in there. I'll talk to you tomorrow, honey."

I always dreaded those last few words, because it meant I would soon be left alone to take care of the store and its steady flow of the drunks and crackheads. Although I trusted her and Tommy, and their belief in me was reassuring, I was still afraid that I wouldn't be able to handle the store alone. Before Tommy left, managing the store had always been a two-person job; even Mama Jean never worked it alone. But now that he was in jail, I ended up closing the store by myself most nights.

"Alright, baby, I'm going now," she said. "Remember, if anyone calls, tell them I had to go to the bathroom or that I went to get us something to eat. I don't have a phone number to leave with you, but I know you will be fine. I love you baby."

Like Tommy, Mama Jean made me want to please her, to do the best I could, whether it was running the store, preparing her granddaughter for a pageant, or taking care of household needs. My history with my family and my therapy with Joe Ed was beginning to make me question my ability to determine what love really meant. I felt so unlovable most of the time and I wasn't sure I could even tell fake love from real love. Regardless, I still wanted to believe that Mama Jean loved me.

"I love you too," I responded. "Please be careful and don't worry about a thing. I've got it covered here."

I almost choked each time I said those last few words. Each night as she left, I repeated them over and over to myself: "I've got it covered here."

Chapter 24

It was May 1994, and it was the last day of my tenth grade year. I was so happy after finishing my last exam. I planned to spend as much time as I could at Tasha's house that summer, swimming in her pool, or driving around with Megan, Amanda, and Perry.

"I am so glad summer is here!" I announced as I walked into the living room.

"Come sit down with me," Mama Jean said in an unusually flat tone. "I have something I need to talk to you about."

The cold look in her eyes made me nervous and instead of sitting down, I paced back and forth across the floor, running my hands through my hair while I waited for her to tell me what was happening.

"Mike and I have decided to get married," she said at last. I was surprised by this; I never thought her relationship with Mike was very serious. I always assumed she was too afraid of what Tommy might do if he found out they were seeing each other.

"Tommy found out about us, and he's mad," she continued, confirming my suspicions. "He doesn't want me back at the store… which means you won't need to be there either."

I didn't mind the idea of not having to work at the Buzy Bee anymore, but aside from that piece of good news, my stomach dropped. I could already tell where this conversation was heading.

"Mike and I just want to live our lives and be free," she said. "Mike doesn't think it's right that we have to raise you. And Cheryl and Wayne don't want the responsibility. They already have Holly, and Wayne's two other teenage daughters."

"I don't want you to think I'm just kicking you out," she said. "You can have a couple of weeks to find somewhere to stay."

She looked me right in the eye as she said this, no hint of remorse or empathy while she let me know I was a nuisance. But she must have been a little embarrassed, too, because she immediately backpedaled.

"I want you to know that I still love you, though."

"You're telling me that I can't live here anymore?" I stood in the middle of the living room and yelled at her. "And that I no longer have a job? And *then* you tell me you *love me*?"

What had I done that was so bad, other than look after Holly, do chores around the house, and work in numerous dangerous situations at the Buzy Bee, all for just room and board? I was furious, and hurt, and confused.

"You will have your freedom back in a few minutes!" I ran upstairs to my room in the attic and began throwing wadded masses of clothes into a black plastic trash bag, all the while wondering where I would go or how I would get there. Tasha and Megan were both attending graduation ceremonies that night and I didn't want to ruin their plans.

Mrs. Ellis. My study hall teacher. *If you ever need me, you call me*, she had said.

I dialed her number and hung up three times before I finally got the nerve to go through with it.

One ring. Two rings. "Hello?" she answered.

"I need you… I need you to come get me…" I was crying so hard that she could barely understand me.

"Angie? Are you okay? Where are you?"

"I'm at home, but it's not my home now," I sobbed. "I'm so sorry, but I really need you."

"I will be right there!"

It was less than fifteen minutes before she pulled into the drive. I threw the garbage bags in her backseat and I climbed into the front, ugly crying and trembling uncontrollably. I was broken and she knew it.

After we got to her house, she led me to the living room and sat down next to me on the couch. I was still crying too hard to talk. She wrapped her arms around me and rocked me back and forth like an infant.

"It's okay, it's okay, precious child. Can you tell me what happened?"

I looked up at her, into her eyes filled with worry, tears illuminating their crystal blue. I tried to speak, but the words would not come. The knife in my heart felt like it extended into my throat, cutting off my speech. The last time I had been this distraught was the day I fell to my knees begging for mercy in that desolate gravel lot, the day Lisa kicked me out.

Two hours passed before I was able to form words instead of wailing noises. I finally told Mrs. Ellis what had happened with Mama Jean.

"Angie, you weren't safe there," she said. "I'm glad you are out. You can stay here and we will figure something out."

That night, to avoid my nightmares, I fought sleep like it was a demon itself. Mrs. Ellis sat by me on the couch and drew me close to her. We watched TV in silence until it was time for bed.

"Angie," she whispered. "Honey, you need to get in bed where you will be comfortable. I'll get you tucked in and you will be safe."

I liked the couch. I felt safe there, a place of refuge and comfort. It reminded of when I was little and Memaw would pry me away from the window forcing me to give up the search for my mama every night. Except now I knew that no one was coming for me. That night, my mind was filled with a new worry.

I began to worry that, after sharing some of my deepest secrets with Mrs. Ellis and her husband, they would begin to despise me like everyone else had. I loved them too much and could not bear the thought of rejection again. At the end of two weeks of staying with them, I decided it was time to devise a plan and I had to do it quickly.

As soon as I heard her in the kitchen preparing breakfast one morning, I crawled out of bed and gathered my few belongings. I followed the smell of her wonderful cooking into the kitchen.

"Good morning, sweetheart," she said with a big smile on her face.

"Morning," I said as I walked over and wrapped my arms around her, laying my head on her shoulder.

"Are you hungry? Breakfast is almost ready."

I wasn't really hungry, but I was sure I wanted to sit with her one last time and etch into my memory the kindness of her face and the softness of her voice. I put on my bravest face as we ate and began to chat.

"Thank you for getting me the other day and letting me stay here. I'm really sorry I was so dramatic and I hope I didn't cause you too much trouble."

I felt the pain welling in my throat again, but knew I had to stay strong. I began to speak several times before I could actually get the words out.

"I talked to my friend Megan this morning. If you don't mind, you can just drop me off at her house today." That was as far as I could get without breaking down.

"What?" She tilted her head, looking as though she was about to cry. "What are your plans? Angie, I can't just drop you off somewhere not knowing that you are okay. Have you lived there before?"

"No ma'am," I said through a forced smile. "I haven't lived there before, but Megan says I can stay for a while, and I have some other friends, too. I will be okay."

Around noon we got into Mrs. Ellis' white Crown Victoria and drove five minutes to Megan's house. I knew as I got out this would be the last time I would see Mrs. Ellis for a while, since school was out for the summer. She got out of the car and hugged me as tight as she could.

"Angie, I really don't want to leave you here. Are you sure about this?"

I wanted to tell her the truth. *No, I'm not okay. I am scared to death. But everyone who has said they loved me has thrown me away. My mom was right. I am a useless, horrible creature and I repulse people. I was born a sin child and I will **never** be loved.*

I wanted so badly to tell her all of these things, but I thought I knew the consequences if I did. If she thought I couldn't manage myself, I might be put in state custody, or institutionalized. I couldn't bear the thought of being ripped away from my friends again, from Mrs. Ellis and the other people at Tupelo High who showed that they accepted me. So instead I pasted a giant beauty-pageant smile on my face.

"Yes ma'am. I will be just fine."

The Body: 4

After a few minutes, the coroner came back in with some forms. She showed me Lisa's driver's license, an image of my mom smirking out at me in front of a blue background. It was issued to Lisa Ann Spears, her married name, but she had signed it 'Leslie Spears.'

Lisa often changed her name as she moved from place to place. Not only had she taken the last names of each of her eleven husbands, but she also went under different first names from time to time in an effort to evade debt collectors and people she'd screwed over. She was clever at manipulating people with words. One day, when I was a child, I heard her on the phone with a bill collector. She began to cry, saying that her father was a truck driver in Michigan and that he'd recently hit a Volkswagen, killing an entire family, and that she was still dealing with the stress and fallout from the accident. But none of that was true.

She had also told me, many times, that she was on the verge of death. One time it was a spot on her lungs the size of a quarter. Another time it was a brain tumor and that she'd be blind within six months. I never knew why she lied. Was it for the enjoyment of watching me be overcome with grief when I learned she had months to live? A need to be the center of attention? Or was it a compulsion?

Sometimes her stories about death were true, though. I remember when she told me her tenth husband, Charles Murray, was dying from cancer.

"I hope he makes it six months," she said. "We have to be married at least that long before I can collect his life insurance."

He died after seven months and Lisa bought Scotty and Niki new cars. She promised me some money, too, but I never saw it. This was life with Lisa – never knowing what to believe, what to expect. I'd grown up believing Eddie Leech was my father, until she swept the rug out from under me with a story about Daniel Miller, her true love that was taken from her, and me as the 'sin child.' Is this why she hated me? Because she connected me with the death of her first love? Or was that also a lie, the truth hidden somewhere underneath the layers of all her stories, waiting for me to unearth it?

Now that she was gone, I'd never know.

Chapter 25

I had lied to Mrs. Ellis. I wasn't fine... not really. I just moved from one temporary shelter at her house to another temporary shelter with Megan, then Tasha in her family's mansion. But after a couple months, something happened to end that perfect situation.

Tasha and I had just awakened. I was in the shower, shampoo in my hair, when she burst into the bathroom, shrieking and sobbing.

"Angie, I need you to go get my mom," she cried.

I jumped out of the shower immediately without rinsing off. "What's wrong?"

"That bitch. That fucking bitch," she said. "He's on the phone with his girlfriend."

Tasha had talked to me before about how often her mom and dad fought. Her mom thought he was seeing someone else behind her back. Apparently Tasha had picked up the house phone and caught her dad mid-conversation with his lover.

I ran downstairs to find Tasha's mom. "You gotta come upstairs, Tasha needs you."

"What's wrong? Is she sick?" She followed me quickly upstairs.

When we got to Tasha's room, she was walking back and forth across the floor next to her bed, crying, listening with the phone on mute. When she saw her mother, she held the phone out wordlessly.

Her mother listened for a minute or so before throwing the phone on the floor, dragging it from its position on the bedside table, and barreling down the stairs. We followed her to his office, where she jerked the phone from his hand and cleared his entire desk with one arm.

"You bastard," she yelled, sweeping books and other items off his shelves.

"Mom, stop!" Tasha screamed.

"Go back to your room," her mother said. "And pack your clothes."

At that moment, I knew my stay with her family, in her perfect mansion, was over.

Disregarding her order, we followed her mother instead, while she ran from the office to the living room to the kitchen, throwing vases and plates.

"How could you do this to us," she kept shouting, "you son of a bitch."

I just stared at the shattered glass on the ground, wondering how someone could destroy such a beautiful place without a second thought.

When Tasha moved away, I stayed at Megan's again. I had been at her house for almost a solid month before her mom, Lynn, became suspicious about the fact that there was no sign of family members at least calling to check on me.

"How long has it been since you've been home?" Lynn asked one day.

"A little while," I deflected, afraid she would judge me, maybe even tell me to leave, if she knew the truth. "I'm just busy with work and I like to stay around Tupelo."

"Where exactly do you live?"

I took a moment to sort out what to say, but when I looked up, Lynn's compassionate expression told me she already knew the answer.

"You really don't have a place to live, do you?"

Despite her caring tone, this was the first time that I had ever heard it put that bluntly and it stung. After years of ridicule and being judged based on my family, I felt like being basically homeless was a reflection on me. I tried to act brave and pretend that it didn't bother me, but in truth, I felt like I was so much less than my friends. I felt hopeless at times, thinking that I would never be as good as them. Lynn's question made my fears real.

"Who is your family? Where are they?" she continued.

"I don't have a family and I'm perfectly fine on my own," I said, staring her down, hoping that if I acted sassy enough, she'd stop with this line of questioning. I could hardly focus on the words coming from her mouth because my mind was so busy anticipating the worst. If she kicked me out, where would I go next?

"You haven't mentioned your dad," Lynn asked. "Where is he?"

"Well, I grew up thinking one man was my dad, but my mom recently told me that he wasn't… that my real dad is dead and his family would never have anything to do with me either." Any minute, I knew Lynn would tell me the same thing Mama Jean had told me just a couple months before – that she "loved me, but—"

Instead she asked me another question. "Don't you wonder if that's true or not? Don't you want to know?"

The truth was I did want to know. But I also didn't want to be hurt. If they really had rejected me as a young child – if they really had believed an innocent five-year-old was a sin child – then they would surely think so now. At sixteen years old, as a rebellious, angry teen who smoked and drank regularly, and had even began experimenting with marijuana, I was surely filled with sin.

But Lynn was excited about being the father finder and immediately offered to call whatever number we found. I wanted to look for Eddie Leech first, since I grew up knowing him. Maybe if we talked, he could settle any doubt I had. We searched through the phone book and found an Eddie Leech in Pontotoc County.

A woman answered.

"Is this the residence of Eddie Leech?" Lynn asked, sitting next to me on the bed so that I could hear every word on the phone.

"Who wants to know?" a strange woman said angrily.

"I'm a friend of his daughter. My name is Lynn."

"Which damn daughter?" the stranger demanded.

"Angie, Lisa's daughter."

There was silence on the phone and I began to worry that the woman wouldn't let us talk to Eddie, but the strange woman finally summoned him. "Somebody's on the phone sayin' something about Lisa's damn kid."

When Eddie came to the phone, Lynn cut right to the chase. "Is this the Eddie Leech that was married to Lisa Alred?"

"Yeah, is somethin' wrong with Angie?"

"Angie's okay, but she has been staying here with us and I think it would be good if she could see you." A few seconds later, Lynn began writing down detailed directions to his house, and within the hour Megan and I were in her car driving the twenty miles to where he lived.

We pulled into a driveway and saw a small, wood-framed white house surrounded by huge oak trees and an assortment of old rusty cars, lawn mowers and tools.

A man wearing a white, sleeveless T-shirt and faded blue jeans with holes in the knees stepped out the side door of the house. It had been five or six years since I'd seen Eddie Leech. His black hair had more grey in it and his stomach was larger, but he was still the good looking, slightly unkempt guy I remembered picking me up from Mama's house when I was little.

"Come 'ere and give Daddy a hug," he said, holding his arms out. I remembered him holding tight to me when we rode on his Harley Davidson together. While I longed to feel that comfort again, I was hesitant to hug him. My feelings of anger that he had not tried to see me for at least five years trumped my desire to be close to him.

We embraced awkwardly and he led us inside the house where he introduced me to his wife and their five children. They were all dirty, and there were roaches crawling up the wall in the living room where we sat. I was stunned. Luckily Megan picked up the slack and made conversation, trying hard to break the awkwardness that filled the room.

I finally broke my silence. "How's Aunt Tammy?" Tammy, Eddie's sister, was the only woman I had ever seen that was prettier than my mama. When I was very small, I spent weekends with her on occasion. She took me skating and to the movies, and would even let me play in her makeup.

"Hell, she always thought she was better than everybody else," he responded. "I ain't heard from that old heifer in a while."

I wanted to defend Aunt Tammy, who I remembered fondly as being someone who always seemed to understand me without a word, who took care of me more often than Eddie himself did. But I knew the effort wasn't worth the fuss my smart remarks would bring. The purpose of my trip was to get answers. Was he my real father? If he was, I wanted to make peace. I was sure that making unkind comments would make him think I was a brat and further confirm that he didn't want me.

"Where's your sorry-ass mama now?" Eddie asked as his wife shot him an evil eye, probably angry at being reminded of my mother.

"I don't know. I don't see her anymore," I said with bravado. "Don't hear from her either and I don't really care." I didn't know why, but I wanted to earn his respect, for him to see me as an independent individual who was nothing like Mama.

"Well that's good, 'cause she sure don't care too much about you."

I didn't know why he said that – if he was trying to make me feel better or worse – but already I'd had enough. I had hoped for a happy reunion. I thought maybe he would offer me a place to stay, tell me how much he had missed me, or at least ask for my phone number or address so we could keep in touch. But he didn't express any interest in seeing me again; it seemed like talking to me was a chore he had to do. Besides that, he wasn't what I had remembered, the safe, kind dad who took me on rides and bought me ice cream from time to time. Not only was his house a mess, but his wife was downright rude, staring at me with disgust as she puffed away on her cigarettes, lighting one right after another. I knew this wasn't a place I'd be happy living.

The hour that we had been there felt like an entire day. Finally I gave Megan a look, my signal that it was time to go.

"Thank you for meeting with me and having Megan and me in your home," I said, acknowledging both Eddie and his wife.

On our way back into the yard, Eddie hugged me once more, and then said, "Look, I never really knew if you were my kid or not, but you know what they say, if you take a bird and set it free and it flies back to you, it was always yours to begin with. I reckon that makes you mine, 'cause here you are."

It was the corniest thing I ever heard. I put a polite smile on my face and said, "Thank you," but flying away was the only thing on my mind.

Megan and I drove back to her house and told her mom how things went. I grabbed a pillow and stuffed under my purple t-shirt, then took one of Lynn's cigarettes and clenched it between my teeth.

"Come on over here and give yo' daddy a big ole hug," I said in an exaggeratedly gruff voice, trying to make a joke out of how disappointed I was in meeting Eddie Leech. "Awww hell, did Daddy drop some ash in that purty blonde hair? How 'bout we smoke a big ole dooby and drop a few shots to celebrate my little bird flyin' back to me?" I fostered an unhealthy habit trying to make fun of serious situations.

Lynn still looked concerned, even after our laugher.

"I'm much better being on my own than having to rely on someone like that," I assured her.

But Lynn wasn't ready to give up. As soon as we told her how it went with Eddie, she looked in the phone book and found a Dan Miller. We were sitting back on the bed when she dialed the number she had just found. I heard a man answer on the other end.

"Hello?"

"Is this Dan Miller?" Lynn asked. "Yes, it is."

"I don't mean to sound rude sir, but did you have a son named Daniel who died in 1978?"

There was a long pause on the other end of the phone. "Yes, we did."

"Well, Mr. Miller, I believe I may have your granddaughter sitting here next to me. Were you ever made aware that you may have had a grandchild by Daniel?"

I was overcome with emotion. Was I actually hearing the voice of my grandfather? Paranoid about what he would say next, I got up from the bed and left the room to stand in the living area where I could still hear Lynn's voice, but could not hear what was said on the other end. The words 'sin child' rang in my head, as if Mama were standing in front of me reminding me what my paternal grandparents had said. What if he was telling Lynn that on the phone right now?

A few minutes later, Lynn called me back to the bedroom where she still sat cross-legged on the bed.

"They want to meet you. How do you feel about that?"

After a split-second hesitation, I nodded. I was going to meet my grandparents.

Chapter 26

As Megan approached the meeting spot, an old bridge halfway between Tupelo and Okolona, I saw a navy-blue Ford LTD as big as a boat. I wasn't sure whom I expected to get out of such a large car – a basketball player? The Jolly Green Giant? – but the woman who crawled out of the driver's seat was not what I had in mind. She had fair skin, a kind face, and silver hair slicked back underneath a black cap fastened to her head with black bobby pins. Her five-foot frame was nearly as wide as it was tall.

Time seemed to stand still, even with the cars passing by on the busy highway, as I stared at my grandmother. She stared back, looking into my eyes so deeply it felt as though she could see down into my soul. Suddenly, the tiny smile on her face widened and the nervousness I felt in the pit of my stomach turned to happiness.

"So you are Angie," she said.

"Yes, I am."

"My name is Alta, but all the grandchildren call me Grandma Miller," she said in a soft Pennsylvania Dutch accent. "You can call me that, too, if you like."

I held out my hand for a shake instead of a hug, but she pulled me in anyways. Her touch was so gentle; I didn't know if she thought I was contagious or if she thought I may break.

I said goodbye to Megan, got in the car with Grandma Miller, and we began the quiet journey down the road, driving south for about thirty minutes to a small Mennonite community near Okolona.

As we drove, I realized that I recognized the surroundings from a trip my mother had taken me on when I was young. I remembered being at an unfamiliar house, wanting to play with the children in the yard, but not being allowed to. The adults at the house had called the kids back inside, and Mama made me get back in the car. Had she brought me here? Was this the place I was remembering?

I forgot that train of thought when we turned down a rough back road that led us to a doublewide mobile home surrounded by a white picket fence. As we got out of the car, a man with grey hair and a thick grey beard to match appeared from behind the house, looking sternly at us as he walked forward.

"I am Daniel's father, Dan Miller," he said, shaking my hand.

"It's nice to meet you," I said with some hesitation. His eyes did not twinkle like Grandma Miller's; I worried that he would be hard to warm up to. I decided to err on the side of caution and not call him Grandpa at first.

"Thank you for letting me come to visit you, Mr. Miller."

Grandma Miller crawled out of the car behind me.

"Dan, will it be okay for her to call you Grandpa, like the other grandchildren do?" Grandma Miller asked him as she approached.

"I suppose so," he replied, looking at her crossly when she mentioned the other grandchildren. I got the feeling I should wait until I got comfortable calling him something as familiar as 'grandpa.'

But Grandma Miller only smiled, guiding me toward the house with her hand on my back.

When we walked into the mobile home, I noticed that it was very neat and tidy, with embroidered Bible verses hung on the walls, but silent, with no sound of radio or television to break the quiet. Grandma Miller led me into the kitchen, where the table was ready to be set for dinner.

"Let's get you settled in and have supper before everyone starts arriving," she said. "You have several uncles and aunts that live close by and I invited them to come over after we eat."

I had no idea I'd be meeting so many people so soon. I was intimidated, both by the attention and by the meal itself. A delicious-smelling chicken casserole was warming in the oven, and Grandma laid meticulously folded paper napkins and silverware next to the dinner plates. She pointed toward the top cabinet door next to the sink.

"Angie, take three glasses down from that cabinet and fill them with water and ice please."

I set the filled glasses next to each plate on the table as Grandma announced to Grandpa that dinner was ready. As I planted my fork into the delicious-looking casserole, Dan cleared his throat and said, "Not before we pray." I quickly bowed my head, feeling awkward for not being familiar with their family custom.

We ate in silence. Grandpa didn't seem to mind, shoveling his dinner down like someone was going to take it from him. Grandma and I, on the other hand, pushed food around on our plates in between glances at each other. Grandma's eyes twinkled every time I looked at her. I wondered what she was thinking. Did I look like what they had expected? How long had they known about me? And the biggest question, did my mom really try to give me to them when I was five?

Grandpa Miller interrupted my thoughts, glancing at my half-eaten plate.

"Looks like you two are being a little wasteful tonight," he commented. Grandma gave him a disapproving glance then looked over at me.

"It's okay if you can't eat right now, Angie," she said. "I know it's been a big day for you. I will put everything in the refrigerator and we can warm it up later if you get hungry. Let's clean up and get ready for your company."

Grandpa left the table and went and sat in the living room while Grandma and I straightened the kitchen. She washed the dishes while I dried and placed them back in the cabinets. She tried to make small talk, but her voice quivered each time she would make eye contact with me.

As I placed the last dish in the cabinet, she finally spoke.

"I'm glad you're here," she said softly. She ran her hand down my long blonde hair. "You are a lovely girl. I know Daniel would have been so proud of you."

These words made me want to shout with joy and cry with a broken heart at the same time. I had so many questions I wanted to ask about Daniel. What had he been like? Did he know about me? Did I look like him? I wanted so badly to know where I had come from, to have some clarity about my life. But before I could ask anything,

Grandpa Miller announced that the guests had begun to arrive.

Out the window, I saw two vans in the driveway, kids of all sizes spilling out of each vehicle. A silver-haired man, a younger version of my grandfather, stepped out from the driver's side of one of the vehicles, while a tall, stoutly built brunette in a colorful, floral-patterned dress got out of the passenger side.

Grandpa greeted everyone at the front door with the phrase "Welcome here," a phrase I'd never heard before but would soon learn as being particular to Mennonites.

Suddenly, the small living room was filled with fourteen people. I squeezed onto the couch between two of my younger girl cousins and sat, my heart pounding with anxiety, waiting for someone to speak as they scrutinized me.

The silver-haired man, my dad's brother Albert, introduced himself first.

"Call me Bert," he said, shaking my hand. His wife Sharon then enfolded me in a rigid hug, followed by all of their children, sour looks on each face. Their oldest daughter practically recoiled when it came out that we shared the same first name, Angie. I felt like they expected me to melt into a big green puddle like the witch in the *Wizard of Oz*.

But Uncle Mahlon and his wife, Lois, made me feel more comfortable. Mahlon looked like a smaller version of Santa Claus, but with a dark brown beard. His cheeks were rounded and red, and he had the jolliest laugh. Lois was a bit more somber, but her spirit was so gentle that you could feel it even when she wasn't smiling.

They both extended a warm embrace as they looked me over with expressions that mirrored Grandma Miller's, perplexed but happy. Their oldest child, Howard, was four years older than me and took the liberty of introducing himself along with his five younger sisters, all of whom had big grins and twinkly eyes like their dad's. They were the only ones in the room who were not looking at me like I was some type of creature from another planet.

During the course of the evening, the family asked me what felt like a hundred questions. What was my mother like? Where was she? Why was I living at my friend's house and not with my real family? I didn't know how to respond to most of their questions, especially about why I didn't live with my family. It was hard to admit that I was a complete reject. So instead, I began to ask them questions about the rest of the family. I learned that my father had three other siblings who lived out of state. Each sibling had six children, with the exception of my dad's brother Alan, who lived in Tampa, Florida, and had been paralyzed after jumping from a hayloft in an old barn when he was a teenager.

I had a lot of questions about being Mennonite, too. Why did women wear black hats? Why didn't they have television or radio? Were all families required to have six children? But I didn't want to be rude. I made a decision to put my best foot forward this time... to let us get to know each other slowly.

Chapter 27

I spent the rest of that summer staying primarily at Megan's house, getting high with my friends from Tupelo High and new friends I made through my brother. Scotty was living near Okolona now, dealing drugs, and I began to hang out with his friends, Randy and Jay. I had spent so much of my life trying to be the 'perfect' person, and failing miserably. Now at least when I drank or did drugs, I was numb.

Randy was a quiet, kind biracial guy who, like me, had been raised largely by his grandmother. We rode around for hours in his maroon Chevy S-10 pickup truck with cool rims and illegally tinted windows, cruising the backroads of Mississippi. We listened to Snoop Dogg and Bone Thugs-N-Harmony on his huge sound system and drank vodka mixed with Welch's strawberry soda.

Jay was a different story. He was probably about ten years older than me, a well-known drug dealer who had been in prison before and wore two guns tucked in the waist of his jeans. Despite his intimidating reputation, he was always very nice to me, cooking me steaks and burgers, not charging me for the weed I smoked at his house, and never trying anything physical with me. I often spent time while he grilled out, watching TV with him and his three-year-old daughter Abigail.

One day this car pulled up to his house, bass music rattling the illegally tinted windows. A black guy and a white guy got out.

When Jay saw them, he turned to me, "I gotta go take care of some business. Take Abigail into the bedroom and don't come out for anything. If you hear shots, get under the bed." He took out a key and locked the door behind us, then went out to the front yard to talk to the guys.

I watched him from the bedroom window. Everything seemed to go smoothly and after a few minutes, he came back in, unlocked the bedroom door, and turned the TV back on without a word.

Interactions like this made me feel like I lived in two different worlds. At the same time as I was getting to know Randy and Jay, I was spending more time with my gentle, law-abiding, and above all wholesome Mennonite family, especially Uncle Mahlon and Aunt Lois. They knew I cursed, drank, and smoked pot. At this point, I carried my bottles of mixed vodka-and-Welch's soda everywhere with me. But they didn't try to change me right away. Aunt Lois told me on several occasions, "I don't know how you turned out as good as you did," always without judgement.

I grew fond of Uncle Mahlon's children, my cousins. At about five, Kari was the youngest of the children and loved being around me during the day. She always wanted to sit next to me at the table or on the couch in the living room. Diana was two years older than me and Loretta was my age. Although they shared a bedroom, each claiming one twin bed, they were happy to invite me into their space on any occasion, laughing and talking with me until the wee hours of the morning. They seemed to enjoy listening to stories of things that my friends and I had done, or about my brother and sister.

By the time the summer neared its end, I knew I had to make some decisions about my future. I'd been staying at Megan's house on and off for about two months but school was starting in a couple of weeks and I needed to know where I would attend. Even though I could run a business, support myself financially, and find my own places to live, I couldn't register myself for school.

I had grown weary of fighting and lying to stay in school and I was sure Megan's mom had not planned on mothering another teenager. I had entertained the idea of asking Mahlon and Lois if I could move in with them, but I didn't want to seem needy or desperate. I also wondered if they would support my desire to go to school. The Mennonite faith typically only believed in going to school until the eighth grade. But since I could remember, I had wanted to be a nurse. I had always liked taking care of people, even when I was forced to look after Scotty and Niki when I was little. To do that, I knew I had to finish high school.

The week before my junior year began, I visited Granny Jack again. It had been nearly a year since I had seen her, Paw, or Memaw, and I missed them, having selectively forgotten Granny Jack's extreme mood swings. But from the moment I showed up, the tension could be cut with a knife. It was nearly impossible to make conversation. No matter what Paw or I said, Granny had a negative comeback. Her mood didn't change my mission, though. After we finished eating supper together, I got the nerve up to ask if I could stay with them again, hoping that she would register me at my old favorite school, Calhoun Academy. I wanted to walk the tiny halls with the bare concrete floors, to smell the sweaty gym with its creaky hardwood basketball court, and to see the '1993 State Champions, 23-0' sign that hung at the top of the wooden bleachers with my name printed on it. Of course, the biggest reason I was excited to return to Calhoun Academy was to see Alison, Megan, and Vonda again, and my favorite teachers Mrs. West and Mrs. Bollinger.

"It's not your bedroom anymore, but you can sleep there if you want to," Granny Jack said in a tone that let me know I had absolutely no possession there. She had cleared all my things out of my bedroom. But all of that was fine with me, as long as I had a place to sleep, food to eat, and an adult to sign me up for school.

Chapter 28

When I got back to Calhoun Academy, I immediately made a new friend, Teresa. She was new to the school and the only other person there who came from a broken home. This was a big deal for me. Most of the friends at Calhoun were from solid, grounded, "Christian" families with moms and dads. I'd spent my life trying to fit in with them, until I went to Tupelo High. In Tupelo, most of my friends had some kind of family troubles. They weren't sheltered or naive about drinking, smoking, or issues at home. When I got back to Calhoun, I felt like I no longer belonged. Teresa was the only one who grounded me. Her single mom owned a pool hall, and her older brother sold pot. Needless to say, she had a wild side, like me. I began staying with her a lot, skipping school and driving to Grenada where there was a store that would sell us beer. We spent most of our evenings drinking beer and cruising backroads. We woke up every morning to smoke cigarettes and chat before we got ready for the day. We lay there smoking and cracking jokes until we hardly had time to get ready for the day.

Despite having a good friend and several places to stay where I was guaranteed hot meals, I felt rootless, worthless, exhausted by the constant fight for love and affection. I couldn't stay with Mahlon and Lois permanently without them knowing what a complete reject I was. Granny Jack made my life miserable in her house, constantly complaining about having to take care of me, even though I took care of myself and paid my own way out of my earnings from my job at Merle Norman. I still missed the Harrisons, I missed my friends from Tupelo, and I missed the father I'd never known. To top it all off, Christmas had come and gone with no sign of Mama. Even after everything she'd done to me, I still hoped to hear from her every single holiday and birthday. Like the year earlier at Mama Jean's house, I fell into a deep depression. The aching in my heart overcame my desire to live and I couldn't stand the thought of waking up to another day, another rejection.

It was January, 1995, one month before my seventeenth birthday.

This time I planned it carefully. I waited until all of Paw's heart medications and sleeping pills were filled. I had read the pill bottles carefully and thought that the sleeping pills would make me fall into a heavy sleep as the heart and blood pressure medications shut my vital organs down. After swallowing all three bottles, I placed a hand-written note on the table next to my bed.

I'm sorry that I have been a burden on everyone for the entire 16 years of my life. I tried hard not to be a burden and I can't bear the thought of being in the way any longer. Please remember that no matter what, I love you all.

At first I felt peaceful, but soon my chest began to pound and my breathing became labored. I began to panic as I realized I should have been falling asleep by now. Convulsions rocked me, my teeth clanged together, and I bit my tongue. Blood began to roll from the corners of my mouth and my body was out of control. I tried to wait it out, but soon fear overcame me. I picked up the phone next to my bed and dialed my aunt Lois' number, hardly able to speak between the clattering of my teeth and the shakiness in my voice.

"Angie, are you alright?" she asked. "What's wrong? Where are you?"

"I took a lot of pills. They are not working right—"

This was all I needed to say.

"Go wake Granny and Paw!" she urged me. But I was even more afraid of what Granny would do to me than I was of dying a miserable, painful death. At least if I waited for the pills to work, I'd die alone, but I knew that if I woke Granny, she would beat me to death with her bare hands.

I hung up the phone, determined to wait it out, but it rang again almost immediately and Paw picked up before I could get to it. Across the hall, I heard Paw waking Granny Jack. In an instant my bedroom door crashed open and Granny Jack ran to my bedside and tugged my convulsing body out of bed.

"You wanna die?" she screamed. "Good! You are going to die at my hand if that's how you want it. But you're not gonna do it in my house!"

I crawled away from her as she followed, kicking me and hitting me in the head. Standing on wobbly legs, I ran for the door that led to the back yard, then collapsed while Granny kept beating me. The commotion – my cries,

Granny's yells – woke Memaw, who still lived in a mobile home out back with Debbie.

After that, things were a blur. Memaw got me into the backseat of her car and she drove me into Okolona, where Uncle Mahlon and Aunt Lois took over driving me to Tupelo, to North Mississippi Medical Center. I lay across the backseat, my head in Aunt Lois' lap, while she urged Mahlon to drive faster.

"Come on, Angie," she said. "Talk to me; squeeze my hand." But I could not respond.

I awoke the next morning connected to tubes and IVs, filled with dread at still being alive. My nurses tried to get me to say it had been an accident – that I didn't really mean to take three entire bottles of pills.

"Why would you do such a thing?" one nurse kept repeating. "Don't you know how horrible it would have been for the person who would have found you?"

I wanted to scream, but I couldn't speak because of the tube in my throat and the pain I felt every time my diaphragm pushed against my broken ribs.

As my eyes tried to focus, Aunt Lois came into view.

"I was so scared, Angie," she said. "And I'm so sorry I let things get this bad for you."

My anger turned to guilt and I tried again to speak, to tell her that it wasn't her fault, that I was so sorry I frightened her. I wanted to assure her that this was all my fault, just like I had been told so many times. But I could not talk.

Instead, I studied her kind, anxious face as she assured me that she and Uncle Mahlon would take me home with them as soon as I got well enough.

Chapter 29

One week later, just as my hospital discharge papers were being completed, Grandma and Grandpa Miller showed up and had a heated discussion with Uncle Mahlon directly outside my door. As soon as I heard what was being said, I knew what I had hoped was too good to be true.

I wouldn't be going home with Mahlon and Lois.

Grandpa Miller put his foot down, as patriarch of the family. "She is a worldly girl," he said. "She'll be a bad influence on your children." He said that I'd be better off with them, where they could keep an eye on me and make sure I didn't corrupt the rest of the grandchildren.

A nurse came in and told me I had two choices now, going home with my paternal grandparents or going to a state facility for children who did not have a home. I had worked my entire life to stay out of orphanages and foster homes, remembering the horrible stories I'd heard about what happened to those kids. Grandpa Miller was resentful that I'd been born out of wedlock, that I tarnished his son's name and memory somehow, but going home with him was better than going back to Granny Jack – where I'd tried to kill myself – or ending up in state care. I didn't want to be trapped behind locked doors.

As soon as I got to Grandpa and Grandma Miller's house, I was assigned a bedroom and given stern instruction that I was not allowed to use the phone or visit any of my aunts, uncles, or cousins without their permission.

"You're a sinner," Grandpa said. "God only forgives sins of those who are baptized in the Mennonite faith. Only Mennonites are truly saved. We can't risk you being around our grandchildren who are saved."

A couple weeks into my stay, Aunt Lois and her daughters came over to invite me to dinner. This was the first time since moving in with my father's parents that I had any hope of going somewhere other than school. But Grandma Miller disapproved of the idea, reminding Lois of what Grandpa had said. Aunt Lois looked like she was near tears. But in the Mennonite faith, women are expected to be submissive to men, and the patriarch of the family has the final say, even over his grown sons. Lois gathered her five girls, leaving abruptly, and I went to my bedroom and sobbed, feeling like a prisoner in solitary confinement.

It didn't help that I didn't know the language. Even though English was their primary language, Grandma and Grandpa Miller were both of Pennsylvania Dutch descent and spoke a version of German. Every time I entered a room, they switched from speaking English to speaking German. What were they saying? Were they upset with me, or ridiculing me? I felt so ostracized, and found myself wishing they'd beat me like Granny Jack rather than leave me out of their conversations.

When they did speak to me, it was to remind me that I was worldly, and that this meant I was different than the rest of the family. This difference was made even starker by the fact that many people in the family called me by my initials, "AR," to distinguish me from Bert and Sharon's daughter Angie. Every time someone called me 'AR,' I cringed with disgust. It made me feel worthless, like I didn't even deserve to be called by my own name. I had seen movies where inmates who had committed horrible crimes were only called by their number, never their name. Was this how the family saw me? Someone unfit to mix with regular society?

Nita Mathis, a social worker who used to live only a few houses down from Memaw's, visited me while I lived there. Like many of the dignified families from Okolona, Mrs. Mathis looked down on my family, especially Mama, and never allowed me to play with her kids. Of course, it probably didn't help her opinion of me that I took revenge by cutting the occasional donut hole in her yard on the blue go-kart. But seeing her only reminded me of an earlier time when I hadn't been judged fit to mix with the good kids.

Now in her visits, she asked me how things were going, how I was doing in school, whether or not I was obeying my grandparents. When my responses displeased her, she rolled her eyes at me, furiously jotting notes on her clipboard.

"No better than your mother," she reprimanded me.

These words ran through my veins like boiling blood. I had never been like my mother. I didn't lie, didn't cheat, and didn't steal. I was still weak from my hospital visit and it hurt to breathe through the ribs Granny Jack had fractured with her beating. But I wanted to punch Mrs. Mathis, to explode and tell her how hard I had tried to overcome the pain and the stigma of being born to someone who loathed my existence. Instead, I stood to leave the room and left her and Grandma Miller with my final words.

"Screw all of you!"

I was so angry, both with myself for screwing up the suicide attempt, and the world in general for rejecting me. I remembered the day that Mama told me who my real father was. *His parents wanted nothing to do with you; they called you a sin child.* I wasn't sure I wanted to know the real truth, but I still asked the question I'd been wanting to ask them since I met them. Why did they want me now? Why hadn't they wanted me when I was five?

I worked up the courage to ask at dinner, my breathing fast and my head swimming. "Did my mom try to give me to you when I was a little girl? Did you ever tell her I was a *sin child*?" My breathing grew faster and my head began to swim.

"Yes, she did," Grandpa answered. "And yes. You were born out of wedlock to two unruly, worldly people, so you are a sin child."

I felt broken and lost any semblance of civilization that I had tried so hard to maintain.

"Do you think that I asked to be born to them?" I screamed, waving my hands around like a mad person. "Or that I have enjoyed living a life where I am constantly being tossed around to whoever will take me for a few days? Do you think that I am grateful for a mother who can't stand the sight of me and a father who is dead? Has anyone *ever* thought about the fact that *none* of that was my fault?"

This was the first time I ever remember feeling that all the bad things in my life weren't my fault. But it was also the first time I had ever shown defiance to my grandparents, and I knew they wouldn't want me after this. I left the table, slamming the door to my bedroom, and crying into my pillow until my head ached with pain.

After less than a month at my grandparents' house, I had had enough. It was time to find my own way, yet again.

Chapter 30

I spent the summer bouncing between different friends and family members, spending most of my time with Teresa and her mom at their tiny, run-down apartment, waiting for my senior year to begin. Despite working half a dozen different jobs, sleeping on people's sofas, and changing school seven times between my ninth and eleventh grade years, I had managed to keep all A's and B's, with the exception of one C in my English class. The idea of walking down the aisle to receive my diploma with everyone else, my senior portrait hanging on the wall of the school for years to come, was a source of pride for me. Not many people in my family had graduated high school, but I was about to do just that. The sense of accomplishment buoyed me. I couldn't wait for graduation, to begin the rest of my life by studying to be a nurse, and senior year seemed to hold infinite possibilities.

It was the weekend of Senior Prom that my world crashed down again. I had gone on a double date with a guy named Jeremy, accompanied by Teresa and her boyfriend. I wore a knee-length turquoise dress with a sequined bodice and chiffon skirt. The junior class had to give speeches about every senior, talking about their accomplishments and personalities. The speech about me compared me to Cinderella.

"We hope for Angie," she said, "that someday someone finds one of her stray, pageant shoes and decides to keep her. And then she'll have a home that she can live happily ever after in."

I was embarrassed, angry, and heartbroken. I also felt like beating the shit out of that girl that night. The idea that everyone saw me as a charity case – that they could laugh at my struggles – was unbearable. I ran out of the school gym, Teresa and Jeremy following behind to comfort me.

I tried to shove down my anger and my hurt by joking.

"I feel like Cinderella running out of the castle to beat the clock before I turn back into a frumpy orphan," I said, laughing with Teresa. We all ended up leaving, driving around and drinking in the limousine that Teresa's mom had rented for us that night. Jeremy made sure I got to bed safely while Teresa and her boyfriend made out in the car. I spent the rest of the weekend getting wasted, not wanting to feel a thing except fun and carefree. Graduation was coming. All I had to do was hold on until that day, and then I could leave.

But the Monday after prom, Coach Cook, the school's principal and basketball coach, called me to his office. My mind raced trying to think of anything I had done or said. The words that spilled from his mouth left me stunned.

"You don't have enough credits to graduate," he said.

"What? How? Graduation is less than two months away!" I exclaimed.

"You did not satisfy a final history credit."

I couldn't understand it. No one had ever said anything to me about credits, school curriculums, or changing schools. To my mind, I had done my job by staying in school, making sure I maintained good grades despite the fact that I was being pushed from place to place. I knew that while most of my friends were attending homecoming dances and high school parties, I was working to support myself. Wasn't that enough?

"It's all because you have changed schools so many times," he said. "I don't know what you were thinking. Not every school curriculum fits together."

"I didn't want to change schools. It wasn't my fault," I said in disbelief. "Isn't there something I can do so that I can graduate?"

"You will have to attend school next year, and take the history class in order to receive a diploma."

"Isn't there some other option?" I pleaded without success.

When he said no, I stormed out of his office, slamming the door so hard that I hoped the glass window would shatter. I couldn't handle the thought of another year at that school among the sneering crowd. All of my friends would be gone, and I'd be left alone to repeat classes, just for one single credit. I cleaned out my locker that stood in the middle of the hallway, gave the door one more slam and drove out of the school parking lot for the last time. There would be no happy graduation ceremony for me and no high school diploma.

It was one of the rare times that I could not stop crying. I drove to the cemetery in Egypt, MS, in the middle of the Mennonite community, where my great-grandfather was buried and sat for two hours trying to pull myself together, but it was useless. I needed someone who loved me, someone who wouldn't hit me or judge me. So I found my way to Aunt Lois' house.

She and Uncle Mahlon listened to me for the next few hours, helping me calm down, stop crying, and think about the future. I told them more about my life than I had ever told anyone, all about the rejection and humiliation and abandonment I'd tried to hide from them.

"You know, Angie," Aunt Lois said, "There's a reason these things have happened to you. There is only one true way to be happy."

"Well, I'm open to suggestions," I said. "Because it damn sure looks like I haven't figured it out yet."

"Your life has always been so complicated because you haven't met God's plan for you," Mahlon said. "But the Mennonite Church is the one true church. With us, you can be saved and have a happy life."

Mahlon and Lois explained the Mennonite faith in greater depth than I had heard before. I already knew that the Mennonites believed they were the only ones going to heaven, but I didn't know why they believed that way. They showed me some books on Mennonite doctrine and belief, which interpreted the Bible according to their faith. I left to be alone and to think about what they'd said.

I rode around with Randy, getting high and drinking our Welch's and vodka, talking about converting to the most extreme faith I'd ever seen. I loved makeup, big hair, fashionable clothes, jewelry, and I relied on my music to make it through the hard times, the way Pete had taught me. If I became Mennonite, I'd have to give all of that up. It felt like selling my soul.

But I was barely eighteen years old, very vulnerable. My life had been nothing short of stressful. I had felt rejection more times than I possibly thought I could bear. And now, my dreams of graduating and becoming a nurse had been shattered. Maybe Uncle Mahlon was right. After all, his family seemed happy. Maybe being a Mennonite was the only way for me to live a good life.

So I gave in, decided it was a choice between killing myself accidentally or on purpose, and trying this new path. I traded my big hair in for slicked back bangs and a small black head covering. My favorite jeans for dresses printed with tiny ugly flowers that hung midway to my calves. My favorite music that got me through every day and every night for the occasional acapella songs from the Mennonite Church Hymnal. And Mahlon and Lois helped me find a family to stay with, the Litweilers, who were known throughout the community as very pious and that could teach me how to be a good Mennonite.

What I didn't know yet was that I had traded one hell in for another.

The Body: 5

As I drove away from the morgue, I felt strangely broken. Leaving Lisa's body behind felt like I was abandoning my mother, which filled me with a nameless guilt I hadn't felt in years.

On Mother's Day, my elementary school teachers always mandated a classroom activity where each child had to make a Mother's Day card. I never wanted to participate, knowing that Lisa would only throw it away. She kept things made by Scotty and Niki, but never from me.

"Don't you want to thank your mother," teachers asked when they caught me doodling instead of making a real card. "Show her how special she is, how wonderful it is that she's your mother?"

But that wasn't how I felt. In fact, when I was younger, I had often wished my mother was dead. Life seemed like it would be easier if she were gone. Not only would I not have to deal with her abuse, but I'd have an explanation for her neglect. After all, if she were dead, nothing would be her fault. And I wouldn't have to wrestle with questions that no child could answer: why did my mother leave me for months at a time? When was she coming back to get me? And, most hurtful of all, why didn't she want me?

As an adult, I had long accepted that the only thing Lisa taught me was how not to parent. She was an example of all the things I didn't want to do with my own daughters. I wanted to be protective, attentive, and affectionate. I wanted my children to know, without a doubt, that I would be there for them, would keep them safe, and that I loved them. When they gave me Mother's Day cards, I cherished them, knowing that they came from the heart.

Now that Lisa was gone, however, my emotions were a confusing blend of sadness and guilt. Although it was of her own doing, I found it sad that her body had lain in that house alone for at least two days before being found. And I felt guilty for all the times I wished she were dead. I found myself wishing that I could find one of those Mother's Day cards… some tangible reminder of the past, of a young girl's devotion to her mother, even if it was unrequited and undeserved.

Chapter 31

Living with the Litweilers, I learned early that the Mennonite culture abided by a strict hierarchy, and that women resided at the bottom, expected to be subservient to their husbands, fathers, and other men in the community. They were not allowed to weigh in on big decisions, like purchasing a car or a house. They were only given a certain allowance to pay for personal items or groceries, and no more. And they were expected to have three meals on the table each day, and to take homemade lunches and dinners into the fields if their husbands were working. I was taught to clean the floors on my hands and knees instead of using a mop.

This did not sit well with me. I had seen my Mennonite grandmother live her life like a puppet on my grandfather's string. While Mahlon treated Lois with more kindness and appreciation than my grandfather treated my grandmother, I was still amazed by how hard Lois worked in the family wood-shop, sanding and staining beds and cabinets on top of preparing three homemade meals every day, with snacks in between. I knew my headstrong nature would not back down easily.

But it wasn't all bad, or lonely. Through Aunt Lois, I met Charlotte Unruh, another young woman, like me, who had grown up outside the faith. She seemed to understand my situation better than the others and was never judgmental of my struggles. We sewed dresses together at her house and invited other Mennonite ladies for lunch potlucks.

Becoming a Mennonite also put me on a fast track to the next phase of my life – being a wife. As soon as I turned eighteen, I was pressured by my Mennonite family to find a husband. Secretly, I didn't want to be married. But whenever I had expressed that, I was ridiculed. So I learned to say what they wanted to hear and in fact began to believe it myself. Marriage seemed to be my only option.

The question – whom I would marry – dominated my mind. At sixteen, a therapist had told me that I had to be very careful when getting into relationships.

"You are likely to be attracted to people just like the ones you have grown up around," she said. "Like the ones who abused you."

That was the most absurd thing I had ever heard. I would be attracted to someone with substance abuse issues like Mama? Anger like Granny Jack? Or, worst of all, someone who would sexually assault me, like Jerry? I was convinced she was off her rocker.

But as it turned out, she was right. I had never been very interested in dating, doing it more from a sense that it was expected than from strong feelings towards anyone. But everyone I had dated in high school was either abusive or had addictive behaviors. Megan had tried to set me up with several guys, but most of the men I met referred to me as their 'bitch' or made fun of me for my sexual inexperience.

The guy I dated the most was a guy I had met at Tupelo High School. He threw me around, grabbing my arm or hitting me at times if I didn't want to have sex. Even while we dated, he hooked up with other girls. He was addicted to cocaine and ended up going to prison years later for dealing drugs.

But the Mennonite method of finding a husband was very different than traditional dating. Most Mennonites lived with their parents until marriage, and did not socialize with the opposite sex other than in-group settings. If a young man and woman met each other and developed an attraction, they would pray for a sign to let them know that this person was 'the one.' The girl had no recourse for starting the relationship, like flirting or asking the guy out or even declaring her feelings. Instead, she had to wait for the young man to talk to his parents and preacher, and then the adults would contact the parents and/or preacher of the girl on the young man's behalf, who would then talk to the young woman to see how she felt.

It seemed bizarre to me, to consider starting the most important relationship of my life by proxy, and without having spent much time with the other party. But I had met John before joining the Mennonite Church, and he had thus far been the most stable form of a boyfriend.

Chapter 32

John and I became engaged in May, only a couple months after I converted. Our Mennonite community, though, did not trust that we could abstain from fornication. Because of what they knew about my mother and since I'd grown up in the secular world, they assumed I would pressure John into having sex with me, my 'worldliness' corrupting him. He had even been excommunicated from the Mennonite church for fornication when we first met, based upon nothing but strict suspicion. So our wedding date was set for six weeks after our engagement.

On June 23, 1996, I was waiting to leave for the church. Over 500 Mennonites had RSVP'd to our wedding, a number which was overwhelming for me, a newcomer to the community. Mennonites showed up to two things, weddings and funerals. This is the only way to expand their social circles and often the only times for the unmarried ones to meet their 'soul mate.' Planning the details had been exhausting, a never-ending stream of questions about who would sit at what table, and the order in which his family would sit in the pews behind us. I had a huge fight with John and his family the evening before. Without my knowledge, they had invited my aunt Kim, Granny Jack's daughter.

Despite her crystal meth addiction, she had made friends with the Mennonite community after I got involved with them. They wanted to seat her at the bride's table with me, thinking that inviting her would help lead her to the true faith as well. Personally, I didn't think my wedding was the time to show my drugged-out aunt salvation.

Even more overwhelming was the fact that I was committing to spend the rest of my life with someone, just because I wanted a stable place to live. My cousin Renee had driven to visit me and attend the wedding. It was the most time I'd gotten to spend with her since her father drove her away the summer before fifth grade, and she'd listened to my doubts over the last two nights. She was unhappy in her home life too. She lived with her strict father and a stepmother who didn't like her very much. We had daydreamed about throwing all our clothes into a bag and heading as fast as we could for the state line. I knew the marriage wasn't really what I wanted, but somehow, I felt as though I had to do it.

The phone rang and Renee handed it to me. "It's John," she said. "Do you want to talk to him?"

I took the phone.

"Hey John," I muttered.

"Hey," he said, sounding depressed. "You don't really want to get married, do you?"

I was taken aback by the bluntness of the question. I wanted to scream, "No, I don't!" but instead I stayed silent, telling myself to breathe, trying to decide if I should tell the truth or lie and say how much I loved him, how excited I was to marry him.

"It doesn't matter. It's too late to turn back now," I said, feeling like I had no other option. I couldn't disappoint my grandparents, Mahlon and Lois, or the rest of the community that had taken me in. Where would I go if they threw me out?

I believe those words shocked him as much as they did me. He stayed silent for a moment, then simply said, "That's what I thought," and hung up.

Renee saw my face. "Angie, it's not too late. You don't have to marry him." I didn't believe her, though. I couldn't let everyone down.

When I made it to the small church crammed with over five hundred Mennonites, I was shocked to see Mama sitting there.

I had expected Memaw and Kim, but no one else from my side of the family. Memaw had told Mama about the wedding and there she was, crammed into the pew directly behind me, drawing attention from everyone around, even the minister. It had been months since I had heard from her. Besides, my entire life she had only showed up to cause problems, embarrassing me, telling people about how she and Granny Jack beat me, or publicly calling me her "worst child."

"Amen," she muttered louder and louder during the homily, words I'd only heard come from her when I was a kid at the church in Caledonia. "Yes, Jesus. My baby is getting married. Praise God!" Every time she spoke up, I felt another bead of sweat roll down my sides. Any second I expected her to embarrass me by breaking out into a full-fledged holy dance, something I'd seen her do once in the past. At least the Mennonites, being who they were, would stay quiet and let her do whatever she wanted to do.

I was relieved when the "I dos" were said and the quietness of the strict Mennonite faith turned to loud chatter at the reception. We had the typical Mennonite wedding meal, ham and turkey sandwiches, pasta salad, Jell-O salad, and plain white cake squares with frosting. Lisa sat with John and me, rambling about how much she loved me and how excited she was that I was marrying someone who grew up just like my dad. She kept talking about Daniel Miller, saying how much she had loved him and how much she missed him.

Every word from her ratcheted my anxiety level higher. What embarrassing thing would she say? Would she cause a scene physically? There was no drinking at a Mennonite wedding, and I felt like I was going to explode before getting out of there. We had tons of gifts to open, but I wasn't interested. I was ready to leave, to go with my new husband on our honeymoon and start our new lives together, far away from Lisa and everything she represented. Even if I wasn't particularly excited to marry John, he represented a kind of freedom I'd never had – the chance to make my own choices, to finally be an adult out of the clutches of anyone who could control me.

We ended up saving our gift-opening for later, leaving immediately after the reception for our honeymoon in Orange Beach, AL. It had been a long day, so we drove to Meridian, MS and stopped for the night. We had never spent an entire night together, so I was nervous and exhausted after a long week of entertaining guests who came for the wedding and meeting all of his extremely large family. I wanted to crawl in bed and just go to sleep. But John informed me that I was now his wife and that I would learn to be submissive and do as he asked.

"In my home, you'll follow my rules," he said, describing only some of the things he expected from a wife.

That was my first clue that marriage to John was going to be a long, hard journey. But I had been a pageant queen. No matter what was going on behind closed doors, I resolved to smile.

Chapter 33

John and I moved into a small mobile home that we bought, located on a deeply wooded section of rental property. He kept up his landscaping business, and I worked as his bookkeeper. I also babysat for a one-year-old girl who was dropped off at our house every morning. John didn't allow me to work outside the home and we had no close neighbors. The only social events I was allowed to attend were the ones that he planned. Over time, I became a recluse to society, to my friends. The Mennonite culture had promised me a life filled with happiness, love, and family, but I felt lonelier than ever. My marriage – the thing I'd hoped would offer me freedom – constrained me just as much as living with my grandparents.

My old dreams of becoming a nurse seemed even more impossible under these circumstances. How was I supposed to complete my GED, much less go to college, if my entire life consisted of waiting on John? On top of all that, John's parents were already pushing for a grandchild. "If you have a baby, it will make your marriage stronger," his mother told me, having noticed that I was withdrawn and guarded, and that John seemed curt and unhappy.

I was only nineteen; I had so many things I wanted to do with my life, so many things I still hoped to experience. My biggest fear was that I would turn out like Mama, become cold, angry, and abusive. I loved my baby-sitting job and treated the child as good as I would my own, but it was still a job, and at the end of the day, I could send her home. What would I be like with my own children, when I couldn't send them anywhere? I couldn't bear the thought of abandoning them like Mama had with me.

But after a year of constant pressure, I finally visited the OBGYN to discuss the possibility of pregnancy. The physician told me it would take 6 months to a year to get pregnant after stopping birth control. I conceived just shortly after that visit and my time to prepare was cut short. In October of 1997 I learned I was pregnant.

Dr. John Seay had been my doctor for nearly two years and, in addition to being strikingly handsome, with a tall frame and dark hair greying at the temples, was known as one of the best OBGYNs in the North Mississippi area. His nurse, Rubye, was equally wonderful, always kind and supportive during my entire pregnancy.

When the image of the sonogram came up on the monitor, Dr. Seay's face lit up with glee.

"Oh my goodness!" he said, showing us the image. I had no idea what I was looking at. "Rubye, will you go to the waiting room and tell her husband to get back here?"

I thought it was only to show John that the baby was healthy, but as soon as he entered the room, Dr. Seay explained what was on the monitor.

"I wanted you to both be here to see this," he said. "Twins!"

It took a minute for me to see that there were two blobs on the screen instead of one.

"Two boys," John said, staring at the monitor.

"We don't know the sex just yet—" Dr. Seay began to say, but John cut him off. "I'm going to have two sons." John looked at me, certainty written across his face. I knew that Mennonite men preferred sons to carry on their family name and the family business, often farming, construction, or woodworking. I said nothing, secretly hoping the babies were girls. Something about the idea of having girls felt safer, more manageable, to me.

My pregnancy was very difficult. My morning sickness extended through the entire day, vomiting every time I put something in my mouth. By the time I was two months pregnant, my arms were bruised from receiving periodic IV fluids due to dehydration. In December, when I'd been pregnant for four months, I had been so sick that I hadn't even gained any weight, my arms and legs, thin and fragile-looking, but my face, hands, and feet, puffy and swollen. When I couldn't join John and his friends for a trip to Nashville, he screamed at me, shaking me and flinging me to the living room floor. After that, I began having cramping pains that didn't seem to go away.

Later that week when I went for my routine prenatal visit, Dr. Seay informed me that my blood pressure was significantly elevated and that the babies' heart rates had changed, along with some other things that I didn't understand at the time. Their advice was to go home and go straight to bed, to take it easy on myself.

"The only reason you should get out of the bed should be to go to the bathroom," Dr. Seay said. "Don't even stand long enough to shower, just take lukewarm baths instead. And I want to see you every week until your blood pressure is under control!"

John was furious when he came home to find me lying in bed. After seeing the sonogram and learning that both babies were girls, John had never attended another doctor's visit with me. He was convinced that the sonogram technician surely didn't know what she was doing. He had argued with her that at least one of the babies had to be a boy. He also did not believe me when I told him Dr. Seay had placed me on bedrest. First he thought I was lying, then insisted that my doctor was crazy and that we had planned this scheme so that I didn't have to do anything. He ridiculed me for not maintaining the cooking and cleaning.

I didn't tell anyone about the argument John and I had that week or about him knocking me to the ground, worried that they wouldn't believe me or worse, that they would blame me. Before my pregnancy, John had never touched me like this and, after two years of not experiencing this kind of physical abuse, I felt like I must be going crazy. I began to have flashbacks to being hit by Lisa, by Granny Jack. I had learned as a child how to handle the abuse of other adults around me, but this was my first experience as a grown woman being abused by her spouse, the person who was supposed to be my counterpart. It was also the first time other lives were at stake.

I had not been able to sleep well since the encounter, struggling with severe nightmares. I was so angry that I could not close my eyes without seeing things that haunted me from my past, and the intensity of my feelings made me wonder if the babies I was carrying could feel the emotional and physical pain I was feeling. I tried hard to think of good things, to protect them from what I was feeling. Joe Ed Morris, and the cassette tape he had given me when I was sixteen, came into my mind.

There is cool air blowing on my head. There is warm blood running through my veins. I am safe. I am not afraid.

Everything came to a head when Errol Wedel, the Mennonite minister, and his wife visited me. Instead of asking about my illness or offering to help, they scolded me for wearing pajamas instead of my dress and head covering, and for not attending church.

"It doesn't matter what the doctors say," Minister Wedel said. "God is a higher power than any doctor and nothing should stand in our way of being at church."

His wife spoke up. "We can put a chair in the very back of the sanctuary for you in case you get sick during the service, but you are the only one to blame for your absence at church."

I had tried so hard to abide by the man-made rules of the Mennonite faith, but I had finally had enough. As I sat in my own living room listening to how I was sinful for abiding by doctor's orders over God's demands, I wondered to myself how I would ever ensure that my children would not grow up like this.

"If I go to hell because I am trying to protect myself and my unborn babies from dying," I said, too angry to be nervous about speaking to the minister this way, "I promise to save a seat for all of you hypocrites who sit and judge everybody. Hell can't be any worse than putting up with you people!"

The room fell silent as I slammed my bedroom door behind me.

I got multiple phone calls from wives of deacons and other acquaintances from church in response to my blow up with the minister. Everyone told me how they only had my best interest at heart, but that ignoring the doctor and abiding by the rules of the church was the right thing to do.

I didn't care. It had felt good to speak up, like a new sense of empowerment. I was no longer just defending myself, I was defending the two lives growing inside me, whose well-being depended solely on me.

That night I lay in bed thinking about everything I'd been promised if I only became a Mennonite. About the Mennonite doctrine book, with its man-made rules. About how people sitting in my living room degraded doctors of great intelligence. And I questioned why I had ever allowed myself to be pulled in. I felt like I had been brainwashed and I was not going to let this go on any longer.

I broke the news to John when he came to bed that night.

"I can't do this whole Mennonite thing anymore. I want out."

To my surprise, John felt the same way. A big fan of music and TV, he had hated the church growing up and had resented living by other people's rules. He was finally ready to leave.

This was the first and last time we agreed on anything since we were married.

Chapter 34

When Nurse Rubye entered the room for my thirty-week appointment, she greeted me and my friend Charlotte with her usual contagious lightheartedness, chatting as she placed the blood pressure cuff on my arm and pumped air into it. But her smile quickly turned to panic.

"Are you dizzy at all?" she asked frantically. "Have you had any chest pain or any unusual pain?"

I began to tell her what an awful night I had and how tired I was but she was already heading for the door.

"I have to get the doctor in here right away," she said. "Your blood pressure is 210 over 128."

Within seconds Rubye was back in the room with a doctor by her side working like mad, one placing monitor leads on my chest and the other placing a monitor belt around my stomach. Charlotte stood in the corner with a look of horror on her face. This had never happened before and I was confused and frightened.

"What's going on?" I asked. "Are the babies okay?" They didn't hear me.

"Someone tell me what's happening!" I demanded.

"Your blood pressure is so high you could have a stroke and you're in labor, Angie," the doctor said firmly as he continued messing with the monitor around my protruding abdomen. "Rubye, call the ambulance and get her to the hospital."

Once I was in the labor and delivery area, I was swarmed with a team of nurses and doctors all performing different procedures. One nurse started an IV in my arm while the doctor told me to put my feet into the stirrups and spread my knees apart.

"She's dilated four centimeters," the doctor said. "But it's too soon. We need to stop the labor."

They gave me medication to stop my labor. I was sweating, begging for fans, and wanted to sit up, but was told I had to lie flat on my back to help decrease the risk of dilating more. Charlotte remained at my bedside, calling John every 30 minutes, but he kept saying he was busy working on his truck and that I would be just fine. Charlotte was growing more frustrated with each call and finally called John's mother, Gloria, who came to the hospital. Once she saw how bad I was doing, she forced John to visit as well.

For nearly two weeks while I remained there in the hospital, John, Gloria, Charlotte, even my cousin Renee, came to visit me, but it didn't help. I was miserable, sweating, with heart palpitations, and only allowed to raise the head of my bed slightly for meals. My face, feet and legs continued to swell and I felt weaker with each passing day.

On March 9, Gloria sat in a chair that was situated at the end of my bed crocheting a baby blanket. I felt worse than I could ever remember, like my chest was so heavy that I couldn't breathe. I sat straight up in bed and began pulling all the monitors off of me, tugging my hospital gown off.

When she saw me doing this, Gloria got up from her chair, running out of the room.

"Someone help!" she screamed in the doorway. "She's turning blue! We need help *now*!"

The next thing I remember is seeing a group of people looking down on me, circling me like vultures with their prey. I wanted to talk, to beg for help, but I couldn't. I couldn't even feel the pain or sickness I had felt for so long. Instead, I went from laying on the bed, looking up at the people above me, to floating above them, and looking back down at myself, feeling total peace.

I would later learn that my toxemia had turned to preeclampsia, endangering my life and the lives of my babies. They were at risk for being so premature, and I had slipped into congestive heart failure. As soon as the medications to stop labor were discontinued, I went back into labor, lasting the entire night. After numerous failed attempts at placing an epidural, I decided to give natural birth.

John was nowhere to be seen, working on a tractor at his father's shop in Okolona, but his parents had called Memaw to let her know that things had taken a turn for the worse. Granny Jack, Paw, and Lisa all came to the hospital. While Granny Jack and Paw stayed in the waiting area, Lisa made a grand entrance, letting the nurses know she was my mother.

"I live in Michigan," she lied to them, attention-seeking as always. "But I flew in as soon as I heard things were getting worse."

I thought I was hallucinating when I heard my mother's voice. At our last conversation, when I'd gone to visit her and her new boyfriend when I was only a few months pregnant, she had accused me of thinking I was too good for them because I had asked Niki to smoke her pot outside.

"You always did think you were better than everybody else," she said. "You'll probably raise your two little brats just the same. If you and your little babies are too good to be in the house with a little pot, then you can leave."

That was the last time I'd seen her. Now I saw her face leaning down over me, drawing closer to me, smelling strongly of smoke. I had already worked to get away from the Mennonite church, to protect myself and my babies. I now knew I needed to do the same with Mama. For the first time, I stopped justifying her actions, stopped coming up with reasons to excuse her abandoning me. The monitor hanging above my bed began buzzing and I could see that my heart rate was increasing rapidly. My nurse, Gail, came in to my rescue.

"Get her out of here," I managed to say. I was relieved to see that, when Mama refused to leave, security escorted her out.

After about 20 hours of labor, my first child, Katie, was born at 9 am. Her cry was nothing like the ones I had heard from other babies being born during my two weeks in the labor and delivery area. Instead of strong wails, she gave out faint, intermittent grunts. Dr. Seay held her up for me to see, her entire body fitting into one hand, before he passed her off to one of the five doctors that were present for this delivery.

I wanted to see what they were doing with her, but I had bigger fish to fry at the moment. Only five minutes later, Chelsea made her grand entrance into the world. She was slightly bigger than Katie, but her skin was much darker, almost blue, and there was no crying or grunting, no noise of any kind.

I tried to see my babies through the crowds that surrounded them, but things turned to black and white again. I heard Dr. Seay calling my name and could even see his eyes, staring directly into mine through the bright light that hung above the bed. Then I passed out.

Chapter 35

It was nearly twenty-four hours until I was well enough to make the wheelchair trip down the hall to the neonatal intensive care unit to see Katie and Chelsea. The doctor tried to prepare me for what I was about to see, telling me there was no way to know what kinds of problems might develop with babies 8 weeks early. They were in open incubators directly across from each other, on ventilators and feeding tubes. There were IV lines and monitoring device wires everywhere, their eyes completely covered with a gold foil-lined mask. Instead of being cuddled like other newborn babies, they both lay motionless, chests rising up and down with the ventilator, no muscle tone in their legs and arms.

Despite this, I thought they were the most beautiful creatures I had ever laid eyes on. I wanted to pick them up and hold them tightly to me, but was only allowed to touch their delicate hands and feet. I was instantly determined to build my strength as quickly as possible, to do whatever necessary to make sure Katie and Chelsea had the best care along the way.

After nearly two weeks, Katie and Chelsea were both breathing on their own and maintaining their body temperature and I was able to hold them for the first time.

All of the sickness that I had experienced melted in an instant. Six weeks later I took them home, Chelsea weighing five pounds and Katie four and a half pounds.

Having two little people to take care all of a sudden wasn't as easy as I thought it would be. They still ate very slowly and only tiny amounts, having to be fed every hour. By the time I would get one fed and changed and bedded down, it would be time to start with the other one. They also had apnea and would stop breathing for seconds at a time.

To ease my mind, the nurses had instructed me in CPR before they were discharged from the hospital, giving me specific instructions on what situations required an emergency room visit.

John was uncomfortable with the babies, having spent very little time visiting them in the hospital. He only changed two diapers before declaring he was done with that particular task, hardly assisted in feedings, and never fed the girls on the night shift. Part of it might have been that he was nervous about how tiny and fragile they were, but another part was just that he was still disappointed that we hadn't had a boy.

"I still can't believe one of them wasn't a boy," he kept saying. "I can't believe you had *two* kids and *both* of them were girls."

The intense feeding schedule took its toll on me; I had never fully recovered from my time in the hospital, and my blood pressure was still too high. Dr. Seay threatened to put me in the hospital if I didn't get help at home. Gloria and John's sister came over to hold the babies and play with them, to fold the laundry or wash bottles on occasion. One of my Mennonite cousins, Paula, came down from

Wisconsin to help me out for a couple of weeks, forcing me to take naps during the day and she got up for all of the nighttime feedings. But once she left, I had to manage grocery shopping with two baby carriers and doctor's appointments on my own. I sat in the doctor's office the day they got their first set of shots, thinking how strange that I was the only person in the waiting area with two babies, yet also the only one who was alone.

I tried to be a good wife and a good mother, but John's impatience and temper that I had experienced from him when I was pregnant had come back. He began demanding a spotless house and a fresh hot meal when he came home from work, accusing me of ignoring his needs when I couldn't provide those things.

One week when the girls were six months old, I had stretched the diaper supply until there were only a few left. I had no money at all; our bank account stayed at zero most of the time. I was looking forward to John's Friday paycheck so that I could go shopping for supplies and diapers. But John had planned to leave work and spend the evening with friends, leaving me worried that he'd spend the money before we got a chance to see it. He always bragged about the strip clubs he visited in Florida, during business trips with his boss.

We got into an argument over the phone. "I'm tired, and I need your help," I yelled.

"People take care of babies every day," he said. "Quit complaining!"

"I'm complaining because we don't have enough diapers or formula, and you're stuffing dollars in between strippers' boobs!" I hung up on him and when the phone rang back, I didn't answer.

An hour later I heard the sound of tires turning sharply into our gravel drive. John stormed through the back door. I had gotten one baby to sleep and was rocking the other while devising a plan to turn the burp cloths I had into diapers.

"Put that damn baby down," he demanded through gritted teeth as he stood, fist clenched by his side.

"Please keep your voice down," I said, hoping my false calm and confidence would pacify the situation. "I just got the other one to sleep."

He grabbed my neck with one hand. "Put her down before you make me hurt both of you!"

I couldn't risk him hurting the baby, so I did as he said. As soon as she was out of my arms, his hands gripped both my shoulders. Before I even had time to think I was slammed into the living room wall.

"I've warned you not to disrespect me!" he screamed.

Katie and Chelsea were both crying now from the playpen, a wailing scream that I had never heard, almost as if they knew what was happening. I moved toward the playpen to scoop them into my arms and comfort them, but John grabbed me by the throat. The harder I tried to break free, the tighter he squeezed until my breaths were cut short. I was forced to give in, to give up, and to apologize for yelling at him on the phone. He slammed me into the wall one more time and walked away, and I rushed to hold my screaming babies.

I had often heard the phrase *a mother loves her children unconditionally.* I never believed that was possible because

Mama had never loved me. Love, I thought, must be a learned trait, and I feared that I would be incapable of being taught. But loving Katie and Chelsea came easy and the fear of being completely responsible for the life and care of the two of them quickly took over. I hadn't protected myself as a child, but now I was determined to protect them.

Chapter 36

With infant twins, I couldn't just pick up and move to another place. I couldn't feed my girls on a modeling gig here or there, or free groceries and gas from a convenient store where I would make no more than minimum wage. So while John's abuse grew over time, I acted more submissive, speaking softly and apologizing each time he criticized me, not complaining when he spent all of his paychecks on tools, guitars, and trips with his friends, trying to keep meals on the table and the house spotless, all in order to protect Katie and Chelsea. Meanwhile, I kept thinking about out how to get us out of there.

I had earned my GED soon after I got married, feeling a determination to have something to show for the twelve years I attended school. My dreams of being a nurse had only gotten more intense during my time in the hospital, as the doctors and nurses saved not only my life but the lives of my two daughters. They showed compassion and concern, two qualities I wanted to emulate. I wanted to help others and make a difference in others' lives the way they had in mine. I thought it to be the most purposeful thing I could do.

Two of the nurses from my labor and delivery, Gail and Julia, had remained in contact with me. They often talked to me about going to nursing school, encouraging me to try it, certain I would succeed. But each time I mentioned the idea to John or his family, it was shot down.

"You have to be smart to go to nursing school," John said.

"You could never pass your boards," some other family members remarked.

"You just need to focus on taking care of your husband and children," Gloria said.

One day, just before Christmas 1998, I took Katie and Chelsea to Aunt Lois' house, telling her I had some shopping I needed to get done. Instead, I drove to Itawamba Community College. I sat in my car and stared at the grounds of the campus, fighting the urge to turn around and drive home. But my thoughts were overtaken by the sound of the screams coming from Katie and Chelsea and the fear of what would happen if I didn't at least try.

When I entered the front office, I was sent to a counselor.

"I'd like to go to nursing school," I said. "But I need to work at a slow pace because I have two small children to take care of."

I expected her to tell me to come back when the girls were older, or that I just couldn't go to college there at all, thinking I was not smart enough. Instead I was stunned by the words that came from her.

"That's no problem," she said. "You can take one class at a time if you need to. Do you want to take a class or two next semester?"

She explained that I could start with online classes and wouldn't even have to come on campus. I wanted to jump across her desk and hug her with the instant joy and relief I felt. Before I walked out of her office, I had officially enrolled in my first two college classes. I imagined running down the hall and shouting, "I'm going to college!" Instead I walked calmly back to my car, smiling and greeting everyone along the way out, vowing to myself that I would not tell anyone until I had completed the classes.

John hated the idea of me going to college. Like the other Mennonites, he had only gone through the eighth grade, and thought, college was useless. For a while, I hid the fact that I was in school, completing assignments while he was at work and stashing my textbooks and notebooks in a box under Katie and Chelsea's bed. But eventually I had to tell him. I had a plan for how I would persuade him. I made a very nice meal and had the table set perfectly, and told him over dinner that I had been working on a surprise for all of us.

"You work so hard," I said, "and I want to help support our family. But I was afraid I wouldn't make it through college so I just started with two classes to see how it went."

He stared at me.

"And I passed!" I smiled at him, hoping he'd be excited. "I am hoping I can take some more classes and go to nursing school."

"The fuck you will!" he said. "You'll stay home with those babies!"

When I tried to reason with him, he got so angry he stormed out, leaving his dinner uneaten.

Later that night he came back to the bedroom, not making eye contact with me. I watched him, worried he would get angry again and try to hurt me. But instead he surprised me.

"If you want to go to college, that's fine," he said sullenly. "You still have to make dinner for me, and take care of Katie and Chelsea. But as long as it doesn't cost me any money, I don't care what you do."

Two years later, in July 2001, I completed my last prerequisite and entered the nursing program at Itawamba in August of 2001.

Money was an issue the whole time. At first I cleaned houses on the side for extra money to pay someone to keep Katie and Chelsea while I went to class, then later worked as a nursing assistant, making minimum wage. John refused to pay for any daycare. And although he said he'd cover our utilities, John often ran up huge debts that we were unable to pay, buying fancy guitars and expensive tools. He once bought a toolbox that cost ten grand, whereas I came home to find that the power had been turned off, and had to pay out of my own meager earnings to turn it back on.

I quickly made two new friends, Heather and Tonya, who became my study partners. At night, I studied after everyone else had gone to bed, often sitting in the middle of the couch with Katie and Chelsea on each side of me, reading textbooks out loud as if I were reading them a bedtime story. When I took anatomy and physiology, I would learn the bones of the body by making them point to the bone on their body and teach them to say the word of the bone.

But with every class that I passed, John's temper seemed to worsen. He hit me, threw rocks at me after pushing off a deck outside, called me names, and even locked me out of my own house. Whenever he began yelling, Katie and Chelsea would sit in the floor on my feet and wrap their arms around my legs, hoping they could stop him. Once, after I called him 'fucking crazy' for spending money we didn't have on a guitar, he grabbed me by the neck and shoved me, smashing my face into the seat of the car.

"You will regret EVER talking to me that way!" he said, pulling the car out of the driveway.

Katie and Chelsea were in the back, secured in their car seats, and had started crying.

"Hush, baby, it's okay," I leaned back to try to calm them, but John slammed me into the side of the door again, hitting my face and pulling my hair.

Finally, he dragged me out of the car and left me standing on the side of a country back road at dusk. I started walking in the direction I thought would lead me to a highway, hoping to find a gas station and call my friend Heather. It was fully dark when I saw John's headlights approaching again. He had come back for me, but only so that I could clean up the car where Katie and Chelsea had vomited out of terror and anxiety.

I had more hate for John at this point than I had ever had for anyone. Seeing my girls so upset and not being able to take care of them hurt me more than anything Jerry or Lisa had ever done. But college had changed me. I had more self-confidence, a pride in my accomplishments that no one could take away from me. I often printed my most recent transcript, looking with pride at credit hours in the 'completed' column. No matter what, my education was something that could not abandon me. For once in my life I felt empowered, and that feeling grew stronger with every class I completed.

One fall morning, a new song came on the radio that sparked my attention. *Don't Let Me Get Me* by Pink.

The lyrics described how I had felt for so long. I had let the words and slander of others dictate my thoughts and my life. The people who repeatedly told me "you are not smart enough," "you are useless," "you are worthless." But I wanted to look in the mirror and see someone better, someone useful and full of purpose. To rise above this, to prove them wrong, to prove that I was worthy of good things, it was up to me and me alone.

Chapter 37

When Katie and Chelsea were three years old, Niki had her second baby, Patrick. I visited them on several occasions, taking Niki shopping to buy Patrick clothes and diapers out of what little money I could scrounge up for myself. I felt so sorry for Patrick, because I saw the lack of drive Niki had to take care of him. I wanted to show her a better way of life, to give her some clues on how to parent.

One cold October afternoon, she showed up to my house with Patrick.

"I need you to help me out," she said. "I need you to take care of Patrick tonight."

Even though I was worried this might become a habit, I couldn't say no. Patrick was nine months old and had asthma; I worried about where he'd end up that night if I turned him away. When she brought him in, I was shocked to see that he was filthy, smelled terrible, and was wearing no socks or shoes. She brought in a bottle that was so stained I could not bear to see him drink from it.

"Here is his nebulizer," she said, handing me some machine. "You just open these little pink tubes and squeeze the medication into the round part. Do this two times tonight and once in the morning. I will be back to get him by 10 am."

At this point, I hadn't studied anything like this and didn't know how this would work. But I gave him his nebulizer treatments as she had directed, then bathed him and dressed him in my girls' baby clothes.

Patrick's cough began to get worsen as the night went on, worrying me and annoying John. By 2 am, Patrick was coughing so hard that he was gasping for air and his lips were turning blue. I rushed him to the nearest ER where he was diagnosed with double pneumonia and admitted to the hospital. When the nurse looked at his nebulizer, the problem became clear.

"This is not medication, this is only saline," the nurse said. "Were there not any clear tubes to mix with the saline?"

Niki hadn't left me anything like that.

I called home and had John leave a note on the door so that Niki would come to the hospital when she came to get him early the next morning. But the entire day went by and she never came. I had to pay a babysitter to look after my children while I was at the hospital with Patrick.

On the third day, Niki finally showed up at the hospital, storming into the room cursing at me for bringing Patrick to the hospital. She ranted at me and Patrick's nurses, while he lay in a tent filled with oxygen, still wheezing with most breaths. I kissed Patrick's forehead and left. A few hours later, I received a follow-up call from a nurse. Niki had taken Patrick out of the hospital against medical advice and the hospital had contacted the Department of Human

Services. Two days after Niki left the hospital with Patrick, he was taken into state custody.

Within a few days, I heard a knock on my back door. Mama had never visited me since I got married, so it was a surprise to see her face. I opened the door, feeling just like I had as a child after not seeing her for months. My joy turned to dread as soon as I saw the wild look in her eye.

"You useless bitch," she began to scream and curse at me. "You think you are so much better than everyone else and now look what you've done! Patrick is in a foster home and it's *all your fault*."

She charged at me, grabbing my arm, but I jerked away from her. Katie and Chelsea had begun to cry in fear and now Lisa turned to threaten them.

"I'll burn this damn house down with you and your kids in it."

I took this threat seriously. Five different houses that Mama had lived in had mysteriously burned; I was even present for one of the burnings. When she talked about fire, I knew she meant what she said.

Seeing the fear in Katie and Chelsea's eyes changed me in an instant, erasing every good thought I had ever tried to hold onto about Mama. Through their eyes, I saw her for what she really was. Someone who had never cared about me. Someone who tortured me. Someone who wanted to see me fail. More than that, I realized that the love and level of protection I had for my daughters had never been there between my mother and me. I had spent my entire life begging my mother to love me, and to never leave me, but this changed everything.

"Leave now and don't *ever* come back!" I walked toward her, letting her see the wild look in my own eyes. "If you ever come near me or my children again, I will have you thrown in jail!"

She spun gravel as she pulled out of the driveway. I immediately composed myself so that I could tend to Katie and Chelsea. I went back into the house and scooped both of them into my arms, holding them tightly, telling them how much I loved them. How I would never leave them. How I would always be there for them no matter what.

Chapter 38

In May 2003, I graduated from Itawamba Community College with my Associate of Science in Nursing degree and was hired as a new graduate nurse at North Mississippi Medical Center, the largest rural hospital in northeast Mississippi. I also continued working part-time at Gilmore Hospital, a small hospital in Amory. I wanted to leave John and move out with the girls as soon as I could afford it. But I didn't make enough money yet. If I could wait six more months until January, I could use any tax refund money to put a deposit down and make the first month's rent on a place for Katie, Chelsea and me.

But shortly after I graduated and got my new job, John beat me, smashing my face into our kitchen countertop and slamming me into the floor for smarting off to him. My face was covered in bruises and I couldn't move my right arm, which felt like it had been broken. It was only my second week of orientation and I couldn't miss work.

When I got into the carpool with the other new graduates, there was no way to hide what had happened. Heather was the first to speak up.

"John did this to you, didn't he?"

I was hesitant to answer, but she already knew and so did everyone else in the car. They all urged me to take Katie and Chelsea and get out that day. Heather insisted that we could stay at her house with her husband, Shane, and her. On the way to work we devised a plan to leave early that day and pack things for me, Katie, and Chelsea, and get out before John arrived home from work. While Heather and I focused on packing clothes for the girls and me, Samantha took things like toilet paper, soap, shampoo, and food from the pantry and refrigerator.

"I hope that son of a bitch takes a big shit when he comes home and can't even wipe his own ass!" Samantha laughed.

By the time John arrived home from work, we were gone and so were as many of our belongings that we could pack into three vehicles. Shane advised me to call him, though, to let him know where we were, saying that without a protective custody order, I might be charged with kidnapping. So a few hours later, John showed up at Heather and Shane's house demanding to talk to me.

They shielded me from John. But within two weeks, he had called enough times to convince me to come back home.

"You can't make it without me," he said. "You never had a home before me, and now you are going to move Katie and Chelsea from place to place like you used to do."

The thought of having to move them around frightened me. That had been the only life I had known growing up. I didn't want that for my daughters. But at home, things continued to worsen. John made me show him my pay stubs so that he would know exactly how much money I had. I began hiding money whenever I could, starting my own checking account at a bank out of town.

By December I had found an apartment in Tupelo, just blocks away from a beautiful park and a great school that Katie and Chelsea could attend. I counted down the days until the income tax return would come, making sure I was the first one at the mailbox every day. When I finally pulled that tax return check from the mailbox, I felt as happy as I did the day I got my acceptance letter to the School of Nursing. I drove straight to Tupelo and paid a deposit and the first month's rent on the first place that I would call my home.

Several friends, including Heather, Samantha, and Billy and Sue, an older couple I had known from back in the day when I worked at Merle Norman, came the very next day to help me move. We packed everything as fast as we could, but we were still working when John got home. He pulled up and immediately saw my boxes piled everywhere and a pick-up truck full of the furniture that I had paid for. He stormed into the house and found me in the master bedroom, packing my shoes.

"I'm gonna break your goddamn back," he yelled, "then kick your fucking brains slap outta' your head, bitch!" He hit me in the center of my back, knocking me to the floor.

Before I could pull myself up, Billy was in the room with a firm grip on John's arm.

"It'll be a cold day in hell before you ever hurt her or those girls again," he said. "Now unless you want me to get that gun out of my truck, I think it's best you leave and let us finish our work."

It was the first time I ever remember anyone directly taking up for me. Billy never left my side for the rest of the day and we finished packing. We carried one more pick-up truckload of things to my new place before I had to go to work for the night shift.

We had packed and labeled boxes with dishes, pots and pans, clothes and nursing uniforms, pictures, and toys. The next day when we arrived to pick up more of our things, it was all gone. John had not only taken my things, he had taken things that belonged to Katie and Chelsea, and refused to tell me where he had taken all of the boxes. I would later learn that he placed everything in a rental storage unit and never paid the bill. Our personal items – including most of Katie and Chelsea's baby photos – were eventually auctioned off.

For the first time in my life I felt complete freedom. I wasn't reliant upon anyone but myself to take care of Katie, Chelsea, and myself. The few hundred dollars I had left in the bank was more money than I ever remembered having at one time. I sat in the living room of our two-bedroom apartment and felt like I owned the world. I felt liberated.

In 2004 I purchased my first home, a small brick house that sat on a coveted two-acre corner lot on a tree-lined street in Tupelo. I loved the fact that I finally had a home that no one could take away. More than that, I knew that no matter what, Katie and Chelsea would never have to worry about where they would fall asleep at night. I even saved enough money to add on a huge bedroom and bathroom and let them select the paint colors. They almost gave me a heart attack, selecting two lime green walls and two bright fuchsia walls, but it was just paint.

What mattered was that my girls and I were safe.

The Body: Part 6

I didn't know what would happen to Lisa's body after I drove away. Would there be a funeral? I doubted it; our family didn't do that. Even my aunt Kim hadn't been given a funeral after committing suicide. But Kim at least had an obituary. Lisa didn't even get one of those. By the time anyone in my family thought about it, a month had passed, and it was deemed too late.

In a way, this book is her obituary. It's also my chance to grapple with the questions she's left behind – and to deal with the fact that I still don't have all the answers.

Chapter 39

The next ten years brought tremendous change for me. I went back to college and in 2007 graduated from the University of North Alabama with a Bachelor of Science in Nursing degree. I loved being able to fulfill my passion as a nurse and was afforded the opportunity to have wonderful jobs. I bought a house to provide a home for my daughters. I assisted in leading a local girl scout troop, taught ballet classes so that my girls could have free lessons, taught choreography to a children's theatrical group, and volunteered at senior living facilities. But I still struggled with nightmares from my childhood. Something as simple as seeing a snakeskin or being waited on by someone who looked like Lisa could send me into a panic attack.

When I was 34 years old, I finally sought counseling on my own. I had worked on a psychiatric unit for abused children and adults for eight years, but never associated myself with any diagnosis I had seen. I had seen other counselors but had been given differing diagnoses, such as anxiety, depression, or mood disorder. When my newly found counselor, Lisa Abstein, told me I had PTSD, I questioned it. Living the way I had for so long had blinded me to the fact that my emotional distress – my anxiety, my depression – was caused by traumatic events in my life.

"Well, did your mother abuse you?" the counselor asked. "No," I answered. "She wasn't strong enough."

"What do you mean, she wasn't strong enough?"

"She never broke any bones, and she hardly ever made me bleed," I answered. The look on the counselor's face said everything.

It had never occurred to me that abuse came in many different forms. My mind had been consumed by the thought that you had to have broken bones, or bloodshed, or severe bruises all over your body for it to be considered abuse.

But abandonment carries its own scars, and Lisa wasn't the only perpetrator. Most of the adults in my life let me down by allowing the other abuse to continue. Lisa knew Jerry was molesting me, and didn't stop him. Memaw sat at the dinner table with us when Lisa withheld food from me and instead of confronting her about it, she slid me food under the table. My aunt Deb told me that when Lisa brought me home from the hospital, a newborn, I was so sick with jaundice they thought I would die. But Lisa didn't seem to care, and nobody stood up to her.

Even adults who were paid to protect me looked the other way. I ran into Mrs. Caples, my high-school advisor, in the grocery store. I was excited to see her, grateful I could appear before her now, healthy and whole, a functioning adult. She appeared overcome by emotion.

"I didn't think you'd live, Angie," she said.

"What do you mean?" I wondered how much she had known about my family situation. But I wasn't prepared for what she said next.

"What they did to you at that store alone, leaving you there at night and making you deal with dangerous criminals," she cried, referring to my job at the Buzy Bee. How had she known about that? And if she did know, why didn't she step in? Questions like these trigger my innate sense of worthlessness as I wonder if I even mattered enough to protect.

In fact, when I looked back at my life, the people who helped me the most were usually people without much of their own personal power. People marginalized by society in one way or another… people who were poor, LGBTQ, or a racial minority. I thought of Pete and Rosa, Dan, the black mothers who brushed my hair when I came in dirty off the playground, and the two women who lived together in the projects. They were the people I owed my life to.

In October 2004, I took a RN supervisor position at a psychiatric residential treatment facility for adolescents. I was responsible for weekend staffing, about 50 employees in all, including LPNs and psychiatric techs.

One of my assistants, Janet Doss, was especially good at her job and great with the patients. She quickly became one of my favorite employees because of her caring attitude toward the patients and loyalty to her job. She was always happy and was the one person who would constantly remain calm in the most stressful of situations. Something about her had always seemed so familiar, bringing peace wherever she went.

A couple of months into my job, Janet found out that I was from Okolona. She told me that she was from Okolona as well and had several children, one about my age and a couple more who were younger than me. She continued to inquire about my family. I skated around the answer, not wanting to talk about my mother to someone who might know her. Instead, I told her about my great-grandmother, Memaw, and then changed the subject.

"Your great-grandmother worked at the blue jean factory, didn't she?" Janet asked. "Is your mama Lisa Alred?"

Alred was my mother's maiden name. Since she had married at the age of 15, if someone knew her by that name, they more than likely knew everything about her. I was immediately terrified that Lisa had slept with Janet's husband or father, had stolen from her, or had done something else terrible. But Janet had a look in her eye that I had not seen before. It was a look of empathy.

"Miss Angie," she said. "You remember when y'all lived in the projects in Okolona?"

My mind flooded with memories and emotions, like a movie skipping scenes in my head. I saw Jerry Bramble's face and that damn snake. I saw Niki as a baby and heard Scotty's sweet laugh. I could almost smell the dirt and sweat as I begged to come inside on a hot summer day. Then I saw the sweet, shining face of the woman that took care of me the most. The woman who washed my clothes, fed me, bathed me, and rocked me just like she did her own children. It was the same face that now stood right before me.

"Y'all lived in the projects with me," she continued. "Miss Angie, I used to take you in and take care of you. You were the sweetest little girl."

Tears formed in my eyes as Janet wrapped her arms around me. Here she stood in front of me, stoic and tall, and still so kind and gentle. It was a miracle, a message from my past that I was loved and cared for, even when I felt most alone.

Now, as a mother of two teenage daughters, I ask myself what I would have done, confronted with the abuse and neglect of a fierce, vulnerable young girl? And how can I best help my own daughters to be strong, to live free of trauma and fear? I've taught them to be aware of their surroundings and some basic self-defense strategies. I've also stressed the importance of open communication.

But perhaps the most important lesson I could give my daughters was the lesson that they can be the authors of their own stories.

One summer day, I took Katie and Chelsea to the zoo. They looked, pointed, and giggled at the beautiful animals, until we came to the "Reptile House."

The reptile house had snakes, but I knew that they were all enclosed behind glass. There would be no way for them to get out. There would also be no one there forcing me to touch them the way Jerry Bramble had with Boey. I wanted to go in and look, to face one of my biggest fears.

It was a slow start. I had barely made it into the door when I saw the first snake behind a glass directly to my right. I became clammy and my breathing felt a little labored. I made it to the second glass case and that was it. I had to get out. That was the easy part. No one was holding me there. I was able to remove myself immediately and within seconds I was out of the reptile house back into the beautiful sunlight and surrounded by the animals that gave me a sense of joy.

That day, I bought a one year pass to the Memphis Zoo and began making trips with the girls at least two times each month. With each visit, I was able to stay in the reptile house longer until, by the end of the year, I could actually stand still in front of the glass cases and watch the slithering reptiles eat. Every extra minute spent there gave me another notch in my belt of empowerment, making me feel strong, helping me claim my history.

Lisa's voice no longer tells me who I am. Neither does Jerry Bramble's, or my Mennonite family's. I am not a sin child. I'm a nurse, a mother, an inventor, a friend. And I'm the author of my own story.